ACTIVE ALGEBRA

ACTIVE ALGEBRA

Strategies and Lessons for Successfully Teaching Linear Relationships

DAN BRUTLAG

Math Solutions
Sausalito, California, USA

Math Solutions
150 Gate 5 Road
Sausalito, California, USA 94965
www.mathsolutions.com

Library of Congress Cataloging-in-Publication Data
Brutlag, Dan.
  Active algebra : Strategies and lessons for successfully teaching linear relationships, grades 7–10 / Dan Brutlag.
    p. cm.
  Includes bibliographical references and index.
  ISBN 978-1-935099-05-5 (alk. paper)
  1. Algebra—Study and teaching. 2. Active learning. I. Title.
  QA159.B78 2009
  512.0071—dc22

                                        2009022067

Editor: Jamie Cross
Production: Melissa L. Inglis-Elliott
Cover design: Wanda Espana/Wee Design Group
Interior design: Creative Pages, Inc.
Composition: Macmillan Publishing Solutions

Printed in the United States of America on acid-free paper
13 12 11 10 09   ML   1 2 3 4 5

A Message from Math Solutions

We at Math Solutions believe that teaching math well calls for increasing our understanding of the math we teach, seeking deeper insights into how children learn mathematics, and refining our lessons to best promote students' learning.

Math Solutions shares classroom-tested lessons and teaching expertise from our faculty of professional development instructors as well as from other respected math educators. Our publications are part of the nationwide effort we've made since 1984 that now includes

- more than five hundred face-to-face professional development programs each year for teachers and administrators in districts across the country;
- annually publishing professional development books, now totaling more than seventy titles and spanning the teaching of all math topics in kindergarten through high school;
- four series of videos for teachers, plus a video for parents, that show math lessons taught in actual classrooms;
- on-site visits to schools to help refine teaching strategies and assess student learning; and
- free online support, including grade-level lessons, book reviews, inservice information, and district feedback, all in our *Math Solutions Online Newsletter.*

For information about all of the products and services we have available, please visit our website at *www.mathsolutions.com*. You can also contact us to discuss math professional development needs by calling (800) 868-9092 or by sending an email to *info@mathsolutions.com*.

We're always eager for your feedback and interested in learning about your particular needs. We look forward to hearing from you.

mathsolutions.com

To my seven granddaughters,
Kalusha, Annabelle, Imani, Olivia, Ali, Madelyn, and Kayla:
May all your mathematics experiences be both meaningful and memorable.

Brief Contents

Contents

Acknowledgments

I want to thank and acknowledge the people who helped me to put this book together. First, two special people without whose help this book would never have been finished: Joan Carlson, for reading every word as it was being written. She offered me invaluable suggestions for clarifying ideas, cleaning up text, and finding and fixing my math errors; and Sherry Fraser, with whom I've spent many hours discussing mathematics teaching and curriculum in the hot tub at our home in Mill Valley, California.

I appreciate all the help the Math Solutions folks gave me: Doris Hirschhorn, for getting this manuscript going at MBA; Jamie Cross, for her sharp editorial work, clear communications, and clever ideas; and Melissa Inglis-Elliott, for coordinating the editing and design for the teacher-friendly layout.

And I have many more folks to thank, including Lori Green and Sylvia Turner, two extraordinary Lincoln High School teachers who tested the first written version of this unit with students and gave me wise feedback to make it more student-friendly, and the students and math department at Sir Francis Drake High School, where I developed this unit while teaching Algebra 1 and Intermediate Algebra. Special thanks to my friends Jennifer Oleson and Michelle Lackney.

Special thanks to my own children, Jake, Matt, and Jeanne, who, while growing up, provided me with intimate knowledge about the evolution of adolescents' brains and from whom I learned far more than I ever taught.

And finally, thanks to the many people of the mathematics education community who made me think and inspired me over the years, including Jo Boaler, Marilyn Burns, Phil Daro, Bill Fisher, Lyle Fisher, Hans Freudenthal, Carole Maples, Evy McPherson, Diane Resek, Sharon Ross, Richard Skemp, Elizabeth Stage, and Dick Stanley.

Introduction

Teachers will not take up attractive sounding ideas, albeit based on extensive research, if these are presented as general principles which leave entirely to them the task of translating them into everyday practice—their classroom lives are too busy and too fragile for this to be possible for all but an outstanding few.

What they need is a variety of living examples of implementation, by teachers with whom they can identify and from whom they can both derive conviction and confidence that they can do better, and see concrete examples of what doing better means in practice.

—Paul J. Black and Dylan Wiliam

Active Learning

Recent research about the adolescent brain validates the educational practices collectively known as *active learning*. Here, *active* refers to brain activity. Learning is active when a large part of the brain is engaged and the use of multiple senses is required. The traditional classroom actions of listening, reading, and writing are only part of active learning. In addition, active learning involves speaking, kinesthetic movement, social interaction, and mental manipulations such as visualizing and imagining.

Active learning attempts to involve the whole brain, which makes it the best approach for teaching big ideas and concepts. When students learn actively in a systematic way, the dendrites in their brains—the branched projections of neurons—make stronger and more extensive connections, resulting in deeper understanding and longer retention.

How can teachers use active learning techniques to make mathematics more meaningful for students? *Active Algebra* is intended to present a living, working example. The lessons in *Active Algebra* are designed to build connections across large areas of the brain, draw upon ideas and skills already within the brain, give the brain a workout at all levels.

The mental math exercises stretch students' short-term memory and recall. Student presentations and group or pair tasks promote verbal communication of mathematical ideas; this verbalization clarifies and anchors ideas within the brain. Writing uses a different part of the brain to anchor ideas; every student is required to communicate solutions and record ideas in a personal notebook. Some of the lessons use physical movement to illustrate abstractions. In Lesson 3, students walk a course at a steady pace. In Lesson 5, students move their arms to show different slopes. Note that it's important to distinguish between movement to teach a concept and movement to practice skills. Many teachers use physical games, such as classroom soccer and row relays, to teach skills. These games can work well but the physical movement required by them is not directly related to the concept being studied—the movement does not help the student understand the ideas. (To read further about brain research and its connection to teaching and learning, see Chapter 6, "Brain Research and Teaching Mathematics.")

Overview

Chapters (Section I)

Active Algebra opens with seven chapters that serve to guide and support teachers' mathematics teaching when using the *Active Algebra* lessons.

Linear Relations Lessons and Assessments (Section II)

The core of *Active Algebra* consists of a ten-lesson unit for students that focuses on understanding linear functions numerically, graphically, and symbolically. Each lesson consists of a set of five mental math problems ("Mental Math Start-up"), three or four Core Problems to do in class, and three or four Additional Problems for homework or in-class work. All problems are formatted so teachers can easily print (see included CD) or photocopy and hand them out to students.

The *Active Algebra* lesson sequence includes both real-life and abstract mathematical situations. The lessons engage students in performing mental arithmetic, writing solutions in individual notebooks, making presentations, working in pairs or groups to accomplish tasks, using graphing calculators for exploration, and creating posters for display. Student assessments are included with the lessons. The first quiz (Quiz A) comes after Lesson 3; the second quiz (Quiz B) comes after Lesson 7. The final assessment of the *Active Algebra* lessons consists of two items: a Linear Equation Poster that students create with partners, and a written exam (Lesson 10) that each student completes individually. (For more information on assessments and grading, see Chapter 1, "Mathematics Classroom Logistics.")

Answers and Teaching Insights (Section III)

Answers for all problems are provided in Section III. This section also includes teaching insights and "From the Classroom" vignettes for each lesson.

Active Algebra Prerequisite Knowledge

The mathematics in the lessons is appropriate for seventh-, eighth-, ninth-, or tenth-grade students who have had some experience solving linear equations and who have done a little work with graphing linear functions in the form $y = mx + b$. *Active Algebra* works especially well for students who have engaged in, or completed, a year of pre-algebra or algebra. The Mental Math arithmetic involves work with fractions, decimals, and percents normally introduced before sixth grade.

Active Algebra: The Teacher's Role

In rote teaching, the teacher's main job is to explain how to do the problems. In active teaching, it's just the opposite: The teacher's job is to get the students to explain how to do the problems. The teacher's role in the ten lessons in this resource is to choose and assign appropriate tasks for students, answer questions and give encouragement to groups and individuals as they work, give feedback on presentations, keep records of individual student progress, and maintain a classroom atmosphere conducive to learning.

Students feel more connected to a subject when the teacher interacts with each student every day at a personal level. Teachers can accomplish many of these interactions while students are busy working in groups. If you use a grading system similar to the one recommended in Chapter 1, you will automatically have a scheduled opportunity for personal interaction with each of your students while you are walking around during class, giving points for completed assignments.

What happens when a problem is assigned that no student can do? It's best not to give in and explain the problem—that's the easy way out and, if done frequently, causes students' thinking to shut down. After all, they know they can just wait and get the answer from the teacher.

If students truly find a problem impossible to do, the teacher has several options besides simply doing the problem for the students, including to:

- ask students questions that clarify the task;

- get other students involved who may be on the right track;

- assign a similar problem modified so that students can solve it (and then reassign the original problem); and/or

- put the problem on hold—give it more time.

Active Algebra: The Students' Role

Using the lessons in this resource, students are expected to work alone and with others to solve problems, make presentations, keep their personal notebooks updated, produce an end-of-unit poster, and complete two quizzes and an end-of-unit exam. Students are expected to respect each others' ideas and use appropriate social skills.

About the "From the Classroom" Vignettes

All of the "From the Classroom" vignettes, such as the one on the following page, describe real incidents that happened in my classroom. Only the names have been changed to protect the innocent. As you read these vignettes, you may recall similar experiences from your own classroom. Perhaps you have dealt successfully with the situations in ways other than mine. If you recognize yourself in a vignette and are willing to share your approach with other teachers, please email me at dan@meaningfulmath.com. I'll post your ideas on my website, *meaningfulmath.com*.

From the Classroom: Adolescent Logic

I use a "double horseshoe" seating arrangement of tables in my classroom. That way, everyone has a clear view of the front for presentations. When we work in groups of four, each pair of students sitting in the front horseshoe simply turns their chairs around and works with the pair behind them.

The bell rings for math class to begin. My seventh graders hustle to their seats. Rose is late, standing by the door talking to a friend.

"Rose, time to sit down and get started," I call.

Rose's chair is on the inside horseshoe of tables. Rather than walking around the outside horseshoe, she decides to vault over the outer row of tables and then slide right down into her chair.

Cool! thinks Jimmy, who is already sitting next to Rose's chair and anticipates her plan.

As Rose slides over the table, Jimmy, with a big smile on his face, pulls her chair away. Crash! Rose lands on the floor and starts to cry.

What does the class do? If you've taught seventh graders for more than a month, you know what happens next: The whole class laughs at Rose.

I, however, am not laughing. I am very concerned that Rose may have been injured. I quickly walk over to her. "Rose, are you okay? Can I help you?"

"Mr. B., get away from me!" Rose yells.

"Are you okay?"

"No! And this is all your fault!" she sobs.

"But how is it my fault?"

"Because *you* told me to sit down!" she shrieks.

Of course. I should have known. I send Rose outside with a friend to settle down. Then I begin class with the lesson's Mental Math.

Adolescent logic such as Rose's may surprise those who don't deal with adolescents on a daily basis. But the truth is that mathematical logic often makes no sense at all to these students. That's why textbook presentations consisting of clear, logical examples and explanations, although necessary, usually are not sufficient to teach mathematics to adolescents. In contrast, *Active Algebra* is designed to help teachers build awareness of adolescents' thinking and behavior.

Connections to NCTM's *Principles and Standards for School Mathematics*

Strand	Grade Level	NCTM Standard	NCTM Expectations	Lesson, Problem, and Description
Algebra	6–8	Understand patterns, relations, and functions	• Represent, analyze, and generalize a variety of patterns with tables, graphs, words, and, when possible, symbolic rules • Relate and compare different forms of representation for a relationship • Identify functions as linear or nonlinear and contrast their properties from tables, graphs, or equations	*Lesson 1, Problems 1, 2, 5, 6; Lesson 2, Problems 1, 2, 3; Lesson 3, Problem 6:* Rate of change in a table and in symbolic rule $y = mx + b$ *Lesson 2, Problems 2, 4; Lesson 3, Problems 1, 2, 3:* Rate of change in a linear graph and in symbolic rule $y = mx + b$ *Lesson 3, Problem 5:* Using graph, formula, and table together in a situation
		Represent and analyze mathematical situations and structures using algebraic symbols	• Explore relationships between symbolic expressions and graphs of lines, paying particular attention to the meaning of *intercept* and *slope* • Use symbolic algebra to represent situations and to solve problems, especially those that involve linear relationships	*Lesson 5, Problems 1, 2, 3; Lesson 6, Problems 1, 2, 3, 5, 6, 7, 8, 9:* Slope in the real world and on linear graphs *Lesson 7, Problems 1, 2:* Relating slope ratio and rate of change *Lesson 4, Problems 1, 5, 6; Lesson 8, Problems 1, 2:* Using constant rate of change and $y = mx + b$ to solve problems

(continued)

Strand	Grade Level	NCTM Standard	NCTM Expectations	Lesson, Problem, and Description
Algebra	6–8		• Recognize and generate equivalent forms for simple algebraic expressions and solve linear equations	*Lesson 1, Problems 3, 4, 7, 8; Lesson 3, Problem 9; Lesson 4, Problems 2, 3, 4:* Solving linear equations with one variable
				Lesson 2, Problem 7; Lesson 7, Problem 1: Solving for a variable in a linear equation with two variables
		Use mathematical models to represent and understand quantitative relationships	• Model and solve contextualized problems using various representations, such as graphs, tables, and equations	*Lessons 1 through 10:* Linear relations in *concrete situations,* including babies' weights, population growth, distance-rate-time, dieting, depreciation, graphing calculator displays, standardized tests, and slopes of roads, ramps, and roofs
				Lesson 3, Problem 7; Lessons 7 through 10: Linear relations in *abstract situations,* including link between slope on a graph and rate of change in a function, links among formula, graph, intercepts, and slope
		Analyze change in various contexts	• Use graphs to analyze the nature of changes in quantities in linear relationships	*Lesson 3, Problem 8:* Interpreting graphs of distance and time
				Lesson 7, Problems 2, 5: Finding rate of change from graph
Algebra	9–12	Understand patterns, relations, and functions	• Analyze functions of one variable by investigating rates of change, intercepts, zeros • Interpret representations of functions of two variables	*Lesson 1, Problems 1, 2, 5, 6; Lesson 2, Problems 1, 2, 3; Lesson 3, Problem 6:* Rate of change in a table and in symbolic rule $y = mx + b$
				Lesson 2, Problems 2, 4; Lesson 3, Problems 1, 2, 3: Rate of change in a linear graph and in symbolic rule $y = mx + b$

Strand	Grade Level	NCTM Standard	NCTM Expectations	Lesson, Problem, and Description
Algebra	9–12			*Lesson 7, Problems 1, 2:* Relating slope ratio and rate of change
				Lesson 4, Problems 1, 5, 6; Lesson 8, Problems 1, 2: Using constant rate of change and $y = mx + b$ to solve problems
		Represent and analyze mathematical situations and structures using algebraic symbols	• Understand the meaning of equivalent forms of expressions, equations, inequalities, and relations • Write equivalent forms of equations, inequalities, and systems of equations and solve them with fluency—mentally or with paper and pencil in simple cases and using technology in all cases • Use symbolic algebra to represent and explain mathematical relationships	*Lesson 2, Problem 7; Lesson 7, Problem 1:* Solving for a variable in a linear equation with two variables *Lesson 1, Problems 3, 4, 7, 8; Lesson 3, Problem 9; Lesson 4, Problems 2, 3, 4:* Solving linear equations with one variable *Lesson 2, Problem 7; Lesson 7, Problem 1:* Solving for a variable in a linear equation with two variables
		Use mathematical models to represent and understand quantitative relationships	• Identify essential quantitative relationships in a situation and determine the class or classes of functions that might model the relationships • Use symbolic expressions, including iterative and recursive forms, to represent relationships arising from various contexts • Draw reasonable conclusions about a situation being modeled	*Lessons 1 through 10:* Recognizing constant rate of change as the invariant in linear relationships; representation of constant rate of change numerically, symbolically, and in graphs and situations
		Analyze change in various contexts	• Approximate and interpret rates of change from graphical and numerical data	*Lesson 2, Problem 1, through Lesson 4:* Finding and using rate of population change from data

(continued)

Strand	Grade Level	NCTM Standard	NCTM Expectations	Lesson, Problem, and Description
				Lesson 3, Problems 1, 2, 8; Lesson 5, Problem 1: Finding and using rate of change from graphs
Number and Operations	6–8	Understand numbers, ways of representing numbers, relationships among numbers, and number systems	• Work flexibly with fractions, decimals, and percents to solve problems	*Lessons 1 through 10:* Contexts of problems include fractions (babies' weights, slopes), decimals (money, fluid measure), percents (mental math tips, sale prices), and wide range of whole numbers (population, weights)
		Compute fluently and make reasonable estimates	• Select appropriate methods and tools for computing with fractions and decimals from among mental computation, estimation, calculators or computers, and paper and pencil, depending on the situation, and apply the selected methods • Develop and analyze algorithms for computing with fractions, decimals, and integers and develop fluency in their use • Develop and use strategies to estimate the results of rational-number computations and judge the reasonableness of the results	*Lessons 1 through 10:* Mental math problems reinforce times tables and algorithms for mental computation and estimation
Data Analysis and Probability	6–8	Develop and evaluate inferences and predictions that are based on data	• Make conjectures about possible relationships between two characteristics of a sample on the basis of scatter plots of the data and approximate lines of fit	*Lesson 2, Problems 1, 2, 4; Lesson 4, Problems 1, 3; Lesson 8, Problem 6:* Given data, making a scatter plot finding the equation of a trend line, and using the equation to interpolate and/ or extrapolate

Strand	Grade Level	NCTM Standard	NCTM Expectations	Lesson, Problem, and Description
Problem Solving	6–12	Problem solving	• Build new mathematical knowledge through problem solving • Solve problems that arise in mathematics and in other contexts • Apply and adapt a variety of appropriate strategies to solve problems • Monitor and reflect on the process of mathematical problem solving	*Lesson 3, Problems 4, 5; Lesson 5, Problem 4; Lesson 8, Problem 8:* Constant rate of change in a new context *Lesson 3, Problem 8:* Using a graph to find distance travelled *Lesson 5, Problem 3:* Figuring out a set of linear equations to make a linear design on a calculator screen
Communication	6–12	Communication	• Organize and consolidate their mathematical thinking through communication • Communicate their mathematical thinking coherently and clearly to peers, teachers, and others • Analyze and evaluate the mathematical thinking and strategies of others • Use the language of mathematics to express mathematical ideas precisely	*Lessons 1 through 8:* Requiring students to work in a group and make presentations to the class, as described in Chapter 3, "Teaching Using Student Presentations," supports the communication standard. *Lessons 8 through 10:* Preparing a poster for others to critique
Connections	6–12	Connections	• Recognize and use connections among mathematical ideas • Understand how mathematical ideas interconnect and build on one another to produce a coherent whole • Recognize and apply mathematics in contexts outside of mathematics	*Lessons 1 through 4:* Connections between pairs of representations *Lessons 4 through 8:* Connections among multiple representations *Lessons 1 through 10:* Connections with the real world are made by using problem situations familiar to the students.

(continued)

Strand	Grade Level	NCTM Standard	NCTM Expectations	Lesson, Problem, and Description
Representation	6–12	Representation	• Create and use representations to organize, record, and communicate mathematical ideas • Select, apply, and translate among mathematical representations to solve problems • Use representations to model and interpret physical, social, and mathematical phenomena	*Lessons 1 through 10:* Using multiple representations of linear relationships (table, graph, formula, situation) is the overall theme of all the *Active Algebra* lessons.

Teaching Active Algebra

OVERVIEW

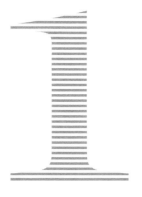

Mathematics Classroom Logistics

The culture of a mathematics classroom depends a lot on the teacher's personality. Do you yearn for something new and exciting to happen every day? Or do you prefer tried and true experiences (routines)? Injecting creativity into your math classroom keeps things fresh and channels adolescent enthusiasm. On the other hand, when you've established classroom routines, you don't have to give as many directions since students know what is expected.

Most successful teachers enjoy putting creativity into their lessons, but they also include regular routines to preserve personal sanity. As a teacher you must decide what regular routines you want to establish for your classroom. Which of these routines do you use in your class?

- a simple method for seating students and taking attendance
- daily warm-ups to begin class
- a regular time pattern for activity flow in a typical class period
- groups of four, changed on a regular basis
- a consistent, simple method for grading and recording grades
- a time-saving scheme for recording grades and keeping track of presentations

Here are some suggestions for integrating the *Active Algebra* lessons with each of these classroom routines.

A simple method for seating students and taking attendance   Assign seating, with a clear seating chart, to make it easy to take attendance. This time-saver also ensures that students have the maximum amount of time to focus on their math lesson.

Daily warm-ups to begin class   Each *Active Algebra* lesson uses mental math problems as warm-ups to start the class. (For more insights on teaching mental math, see Chapter 2.)

A regular time pattern for activity flow in a typical class period Each *Active Algebra* lesson works well for a ninety-minute block or back-to-back double period. If your periods are less than ninety minutes, you can adjust the lessons by either omitting one or two problems from each lesson or extending each lesson into two or more periods. Here is a suggested time pattern for each *Active Algebra* lesson:

Time Pattern for Lessons	
Attendance and mental math exercises	15 min.
Student presentations of the prior lesson's "additional work"	15 min.
Group work on core problems (the teacher circulates, checking students' individual notebooks)	30 min.
Student presentations of core work	25 min.
Additional mental math work	(optional)

Groups of four, changed on a regular basis I recommend putting students into groups of four (or three if numbers don't come out even) using a random method. Change the groups every three or four weeks so that students are grouped with three others who weren't in their previous group.

Emphasize that everyone in the group is responsible for working together to contribute ideas, get results, and help each other learn. For group presentations and assignments, everyone will receive the same grade and thus must contribute. For work in individual notebooks, students may help each other, but each student is responsible for doing and recording the work in his or her own notebook. Ultimately, all students are responsible for their own learning and are dependent on such learning when it comes to exams.

A consistent, simple method for grading For grading the *Active Algebra* lessons, I recommend using a point system. Points are given to each student for the daily assignments, quizzes, poster, end-of-unit assessment, and presentations. Here is the overall point allocation I use for the *Active Algebra* unit:

Lessons Grading Scheme	
Lessons 1 to 9 assignments and unit summary sheet: ten worth 3 points each	30
Quizzes A and B: two worth 10 points each	20
Poster (partners each get the same score)	30
Lesson 10 end-of-unit assessment	50
Total Points	130

I recommend having each student complete daily assignments for *Active Algebra* in a notebook. Spiral-bound or composition workbooks from which pages cannot be removed work well. Instead of collecting the daily work, the teacher circulates during class and grades students' work from the prior lesson. Here is a suggested grading scheme:

Homework Grading Scheme	
3 points	Methods and answers neatly written out for all assigned problems
2 points	Work and answers shown for most problems, but not all
1 point	Work shown for a few problems
0 points	Only one or no problems done

Note: It is important to implement rules regarding the acceptance of late work. In most cases, late work should not be accepted. This rule helps students stay up-to-date, which subsequently gives them a better chance at understanding new material.

A time-saving scheme for recording grades and keeping track of presentations I recommend using a seating chart mapped out on a grid to record grades for each student. (See the three reproducible charts at the end of this chapter.) This chart can be attached to a clipboard to allow you to easily circulate with it through the classroom. I grade the work in each student's notebook daily or every other day during class by writing each student's grade points on his or her notebook and recording the points in the seating chart grid. (See Figure 1–1 on the following page for a typical class seating chart grid after Lesson 4.)

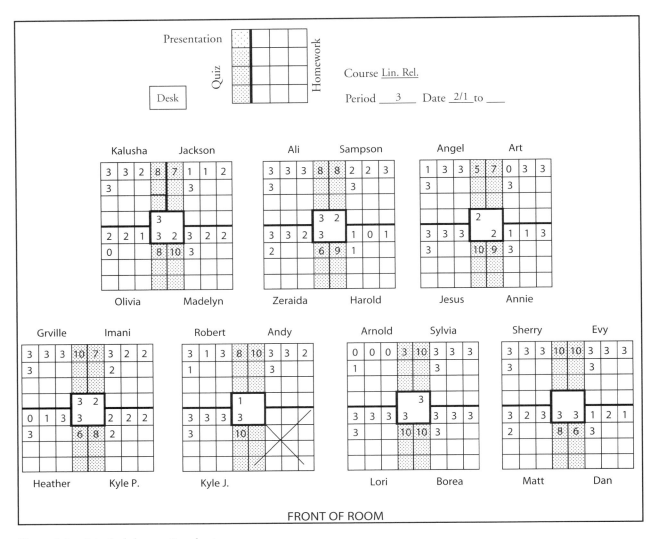

Figure 1–1   *A typical class seating chart.*

On my seating chart, I have a grid for each group and one "master square" to keep track of the date (or lesson number if you prefer) when all homework in the corresponding student squares is graded. For example, the grid in the upper left is for Group 7 (Kalusha, Jackson, Olivia, and Madelyn). I record the daily notebook grades for each student in the wings and the presentation grades for the group in the center square.

In the Group 7 grid I can see that on 2/6 work, Madelyn got a 2 on her notebook, Jackson a 1, Kalusha a 3, and Olivia a 2. I can quickly see that Olivia isn't doing very well. In the center square, I keep track of presentation grades—I can see that Jackson is the only one who hasn't presented yet and must be the Group 7 presenter next time. I add the total of the points in the center square (presentations) as extra credit to everyone's notebook point total. If I happen to give quizzes during the unit, I keep track of those scores in the shaded squares. On the quiz given on 2/10, Madelyn's score was 10.

After three weeks, I add up each student's points, transfer the total to my grade book, and staple the seating chart grade page into my grade book. Reproducible blank seating chart grids are included on the next few pages; each one is designed for a class of approximately thirty students.

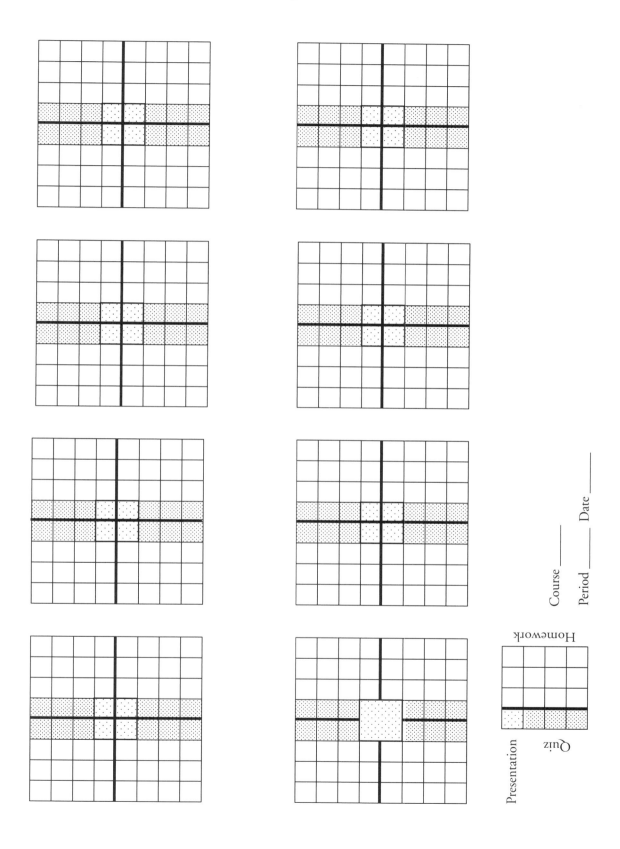

Course _____ Date _____

Period _____

Homework

Presentation   Quiz

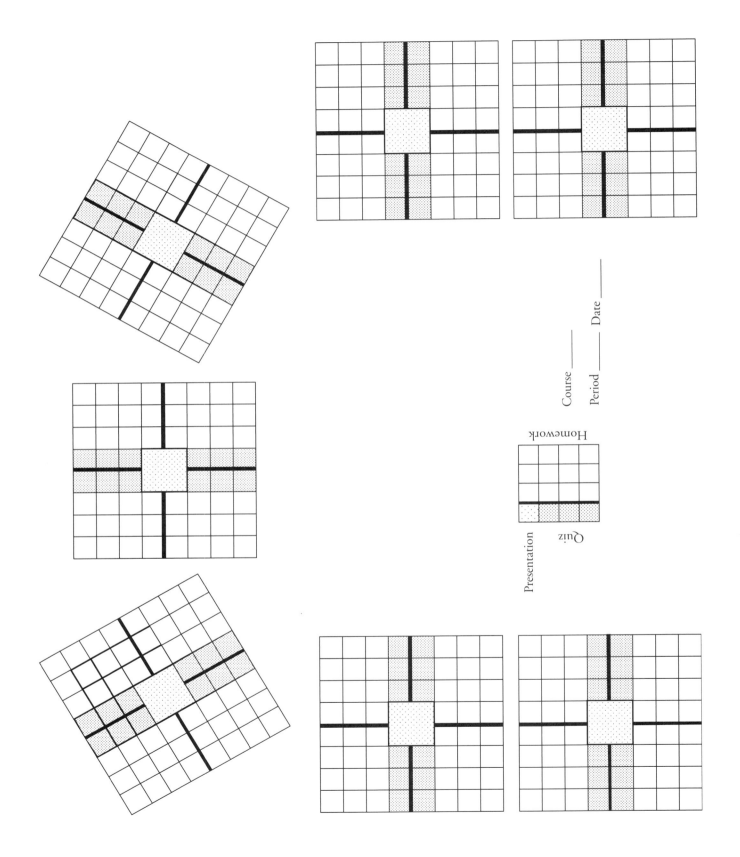

Course _____

Period _____ Date _____

Homework

Presentation

Quiz

Reproducible C
Seating Chart Grid 3

Presentation

Quiz

Homework

Course _____

Period _____ Date _____

Teaching Mental Math

Mental math—the ability to perform simple calculations in your head without paper and pencil—is an essential life skill. Mental math practice gives adolescent brains a workout and provides a review of arithmetic fundamentals necessary for success in algebra and beyond. Plus, it's a productive, easy way to start and/or end your math class.

When I first tell my students *No pencil and paper allowed,* they're frequently surprised. When students are doing math they're usually asked to *show their work* and *write down all the steps.* Working only "in your head" is a welcome change. I explain to students that we will be doing mental math on a regular basis as a low-stress activity to begin each class (and sometimes to end the class if there is time).

Mental math can be difficult for students at first. I remind them that they will get better at it with regular practice—and sure enough, each day their skills improve. (I also notice that my own mental math skills improve!) The problems I start with—finding a sale price, figuring a tip, estimating how long a trip will take—require skills students will use in everyday life. Consequently, you won't hear my students groan, *We'll never use this!*

During our Back to School Night at the end of September, I always have parents do a few mental math problems. They tell me they are delighted I am having their children practice a valuable real-life skill.

When I do mental math, I can feel my brain working. I believe that mental math affects my students' brains in a positive way that is different from paper-and-pencil math.

Teaching Mental Math: Three Steps

So how does one successfully teach mental math? Following are three steps I use to teach mental math in *Active Algebra* lessons.

Steps for Using the Mental Math Start-up Sections of the Lessons

Step 1: Students Mentally Work Through Five Problems

- Ask students to write the numbers 1 through 5 on a piece of paper.

- Explain that they are going to work five math problems in their heads. To do so, they must listen carefully and then solve each problem mentally. They are not allowed to write down the problem. Also, they are not permitted to use calculators or paper-and-pencil calculations.

- Read the first problem aloud two times.

- Allow a short time for students to do the mental math and write *only* the answer on their paper.

- Repeat with the next four problems, reading each aloud and giving students time to mentally solve each.

Step 2: Students Share Answers and Methods Within Groups

- When students have finished Step 1 and have their five answers written down, display the problems so students can see them. Do not reveal the answers or methods for getting the answers!

- Ask students to share their answers within their group and discuss solution methods for each problem.

Step 3: Students Have a Whole-Class Discussion

- For each problem, call on one group of students to give the answer and share one of their mental strategies (tell how they did the problem).

- After the group shares, ask if any other group had a different answer or strategy. Share all strategies.

- Finally, if necessary, add your own strategy. In the rare case that everyone gets the problem wrong, give the correct answer. (See the heading in this section, "Mental Math: Common Questions and Answers," for further guidance on what to do if students don't come up with their own strategies.)

Teaching Mental Math: Variations

Expand the Discussions

If your students have difficulty doing mental math, you may want to start the class with fewer mental math problems each day and spend more time discussing each one. Near the end of class, give a similar set of mental math problems to reinforce learning.

Work in Groups

Have groups work together to do mental math problems. Do not allow written calculations but let students talk out their answers. This works especially well with more complex mental math problems.

Include on Quiz

On a regular math quiz, include mental math problems. Have each student number 1 to 5 at the top of the quiz. Count correct answers as a small part of their total grade.

Mental Math Problems: At-a-Glance

Here is a table specifying some of the mental math problems you'll find in the *Active Algebra* lessons.

Examples of Mental Math Problems	The Core Skill	The Corresponding *Active Algebra* Lessons
Find a 15% tip on a bill of $60.	Find 5%, 10%, 15%, 20% of a number.	Lessons 1 through 9
If $3x = 21$, find x.	Solve "one-step" equations.	Lessons 2 through 9
A pair of jeans usually priced at $80 is on sale for 30% off. What is the sale price?	Given a regular price and a percent off (10%, 20%, 25%, 30%, 40%), find the sale price.	Lessons 3 through 9
You bike 36 miles in 3 hours. What's your average speed?	Solve distance-rate-time problems involving miles per hour and feet per second.	Lessons 4 through 9
If $x = 4$, what is the value of $3x + 2$?	Substitute a value into an expression.	Lessons 5 through 9
If $y = 5x - 10$, what is the x-intercept?	Given a linear equation in $y = mx + b$ form, find the x- and y-intercept.	Lessons 8 and 9

This table contains types of problems you could add to your lessons.

Additional Mental Math Problems	The Core Skill	Teaching Suggestions
What percent is 12 out of 20?	Find what percent one number is of another for benchmark percents.	Use numbers that reduce only to thirds, fourths, eighths, fifths, or tenths.
A $28 shirt is on sale for $\frac{1}{4}$ off. What is the sale price?	Find $\frac{1}{3}$ off or $\frac{1}{4}$ off the sale price.	Pick a fraction denominator that cancels with dollar amount.
Find $\frac{2}{3}$ of 48.	Find a fraction of a whole number.	Pick denominators and numbers that cancel.
Avocados cost 49¢ each. What is the cost of 6?	Multiply a one-digit number by a two-digit number.	Easy mental methods: a. $6 \times 40 = 240$, plus $6 \times 9 = 54$, so the answer is 294. b. $6 \times 50 = 300$, then subtract 6, equaling 294.

Mental Math: Common Questions and Answers

I don't think my students will do mental math. They will either do nothing or cheat. Do you really think it's worth it?

Most students recognize that mental math is a valuable skill outside of school. They want to be able to do it, but they've simply never been given the opportunity to practice it. If you present mental math as a low-stress activity and make it a regular feature of your class, almost all of your students will be willing to try. Let students know that their mental math skills will improve with regular practice. Practicing mental math, particularly at the seventh-, eighth-, and ninth-grade levels, helps students develop the number sense necessary for success in all high school subjects and for life outside of school.

Suppose my students don't come up with good mental math strategies on their own. What can I do?

All mental math problems in the *Active Algebra* lessons involve skills introduced before sixth grade. However, students may have learned to do these problems in a rote manner, using paper and pencil only. Doing these problems mentally requires flexible thinking and a deeper understanding of percents, decimals, and operations. Be patient and allow enough time for each student to write down an answer. Then ask the class if anyone has an easy way to solve it. As students explain their strategies, give them credit for what they already know. If no one in the class comes up with a viable method, you can make up another problem with simpler numbers for them to try. Still no method from the class? Only then should you tell students the "easy way." Give a few practice problems right after sharing your method to make sure everyone understands.

Teaching Using Student Presentations

Adolescents like to talk, especially to each other. Instead of playing the "no talking allowed" game, why not give them something to talk about? When students present how they go about solving math problems, they are actively involved in the teaching process, which results in a lively classroom atmosphere. Student presentations:

- showcase higher-level student thinking;
- transfer the responsibility for explaining from the teacher to the students;
- promote student-to-student verbal communication about mathematics; and
- motivate students to understand the problem.

Teaching Using Student Presentations: Five Steps

Following are the steps I've found key to teaching with student presentations. You may wish to adapt them to make your own system for student presentations.

Step 1: Post and Discuss the Rules

Before any presentations, I share my Presentation Grading Scheme and Rules:

Presentation Grading Scheme	
Points (3 points possible)	**Criteria**
1	Professional appearance of write-up (no graffiti)
1	Clear speaking and explanation
1	Generally, a correct solution

Presentation Rules
1. Each group member must present once before any group member can present twice.
2. All group members must contribute to the write-up.
3. Each group member gets all group presentation points added to his or her total as "extra credit."

I emphasize the "no graffiti" rule the first few times we conduct student presentations. Although extraneous graffiti on write-ups seems fun at first, if left unchecked, it quickly becomes the focus of the presentations and distracts from learning. I tell students that producing professional-looking write-ups is an important skill for work outside of school because many jobs involve making presentations to clients. After students realize that I am serious about deducting points for scribbles such as *Class of 2012 Rules!* and *Go Pirates!*, the tendency to add graffiti ceases.

If you decide to work out your own grading scheme for student presentations, you'll want to ensure it includes the features of the Presentation Grading Scheme above. In particular, successful grading systems for presentations:

- **are simple;**
- **provide immediate feedback;**
- **focus on the method of solution (not just the answer);**
- **count toward only a small part of a student's grade; and**
- **are fair to all.**

Step 2: Ask Students to Prepare Their Presentations

To randomly select a group of students to present each problem, I list the problem numbers on the board. Then, for each problem, I select a playing card with one group's number. In this way, each group is assigned one problem to present.

I also clearly post on the board the time that I expect presentations to begin. As students work in their groups, I periodically check each group's progress to make sure we're on schedule for presentations. If necessary, I adjust the time that I've posted on the board.

Before their presentation, each group writes up their problem and solution using a means that allows the whole class to see it. This saves time during the presentation and keeps the class moving.

Step 3: Prepare the Class for Presentations

It is important to address two items immediately prior to the first student presentation. First, ask the class for their quiet attention. Second, remind students to respect each other's thinking, even if it's incorrect. After all, making an attempt is always better than sitting back and criticizing.

Step 4: Ask Students to Present

One student from each group makes the presentation. After each presentation, ask if any other group did the problem differently or has something to add. Provide an opportunity for students to correct their own errors before grading. Refrain from public praising or pummeling. Instead, ask clarifying questions and paraphrase important points.

Step 5: Grade Each Presentation

When each presentation is over, announce the group's grade (0, 1, 2, or 3) according to the Presentation Grading Scheme. Record the grade and note who presented. I do this on my seating chart grid as described in Chapter 1.

From the Classroom: Playing It Fair When Assigning Problems for Presentations

My students have a strong opinion that life ought to be fair, especially in the classroom. Today we are studying *Active Algebra*, Lesson 4, and it's time to assign groups their problems for presentations. I've written the problem numbers 1 through 6 on the board. In my hand are eight playing cards—an ace card and cards 2 through 8—corresponding with the eight numbered groups in my class. I shuffle the cards.

"OK, Arnold, you cut to make sure this is fair." Arnold and the rest of the class understand that choosing randomly is fair. He cuts the cards.

I hold up the top card: a 7. On the board next to the first problem number I write *Group 7*.

The next card is a 5. On the board next to the second problem number I write *Group 5*.

I continue until all six problems have been assigned to a group. Since there are six problems in this set, only six groups will be presenting. The two groups left out today, who continue to work on Core or Additional Problems, know

they will present next time for sure. That is only fair.

Group 7 calls me over. "Mr. B., we got problem number one. It's way harder than the other ones. That's *not fair*. And none of us know how to do it."

I look at what Group 7 has done in solving the problem so far. "I see it is difficult for you," I comment. However, I know the group has the ability to solve it; they simply need the motivation. "Tell you what. This *is* a hard problem, so you can ask me any questions you want. I'll get you started and then come back later to see if you need any more help. Remember—someone in your group will volunteer to present number one in fifteen minutes. So what do you need to know?"

When students realize they must present their solution, they usually pay more attention to my words. Suddenly, finding the correct answer matters to them.

I continue walking around the room, checking and grading the prior lesson's homework in

(continued)

each student's notebook. After a few minutes I return to Group 7. Olivia hasn't presented a problem yet. It is her turn, and she is getting nervous.

I try to help Olivia—and the group—realize that she is not alone in this endeavor. "Now remember that no matter who presents the problem, you all get the same grade for it. You all need to work on the problem, write it up neatly, and make sure Olivia understands so she can explain it. This way you'll all get a good grade."

In Group 7, Jackson is the strongest math student. As I walk away, I notice that he jumps in to share his solution with the rest of the group. Another student is preparing a write-up for the presentation. And Olivia is listening very carefully. Collaboration at its finest, I note to myself.

Olivia presents the problem flawlessly. I announce that Group 7 has earned a 3—the highest possible mark. The class agrees that this is more than fair. I record the 3 in Group 7's points square, next to Olivia's name.

From the Classroom: Not Fair! Some Groups Work on Presentations While Others Present

Olivia is at the front of the class, beginning the first presentation of the day. I look around the room and see that Group 6 is not paying attention. They are still busy working on the problem they are to present later.

"Group 6, stop working now and give Olivia your full attention, please," I reprimand.

"But we need to finish our write-up so we can present."

"But *now* is the time we are discussing problem one. You'll never have this opportunity again. Once Olivia is done, we'll move on. So stop working and start listening."

Some of the members of Group 6 look up at Olivia, but I can see that Arnold is still absorbed in finalizing Group 6's write-up. What to do? I make a note that I have to come up with a new strategy.

The next day I make the following announcement: "I've noticed that when some groups are presenting, other groups are still working on their write-up. When a problem is being presented, it's important that everyone pay attention. Also, it's not fair if some groups get more time to work on their presentation. So from today onward, all groups presenting must have their write-ups done and placed up on the front table before presentations begin. I'll give you a five-minute warning, and then someone must hand in your group's write-up. Groups who don't have their write-up on the table will get a zero."

Later, when I give the five-minute warning, Group 4 calls me over. "We don't have Part C or D done yet. Can't we have a little more time?" they plead.

"Well, you have five minutes. Whatever you have done, put the write-up on the table by then and at least you'll get some credit." I decide it's important—and fair to everyone—that I stay true to the rule.

The rest of the year, I strictly enforce the rule. (I only had to give a few groups zeroes to get the point across.) In addition to ending the problem of groups working while others presented, the rule had another benefit: it made the presentations run much more quickly because the next group was always ready to present.

Introducing the Graphing Calculator

A graphing calculator needs to be available for each student to use during the *Active Algebra* lessons. Older graphing calculators do just fine. I use a Texas Instruments TI-84, but older models such as the TI-82, TI-81, TI-73, or even other brands, are just as functional.

When I first started using graphing calculators with students, I was concerned that the calculators would "disappear" from my classroom, so I spray-painted the back of each one bright red. Now they are less likely to "walk away."

Before each lesson, I arrange the calculators in stacks of four on a table in front of the room. I label each stack with a corresponding group number (a sticky note works well). As students enter class, one person from each group takes a stack for their group. Five minutes before the end of class, a student from each group returns the stack of calculators to the front table. At the closing bell, only groups whose calculators are on the front table are allowed to leave.

If you've never used graphing calculators with a class, you may want to ask for logistical hints from a math or science teacher who uses them. And while some students may have used graphing calculators daily, others may have come from classrooms in which calculators were not used. To get everyone up to speed, I have students teach each other what they know. To begin, I give each student a Graphing Calculator Basics checklist (available as a reproducible handout on the next page). To check off a skill, students must show a classmate that they can do it. This verification process often becomes a forum for teaching others. As students work, I circulate, keeping a close eye out for items that seem to be presenting difficulty for everyone. I then demonstrate only these difficult skills to the whole class.

Reproducible D
Graphing Calculator Basics

Name _____   Date _____

Show another student that you can do each of these calculator skills. After you perform the skill, have your classmate "sign off" on each item in the space to the right. If any item gives you trouble, ask someone for help!

I can:	The person who saw me do this signed here:
Turn the calculator on and off.	
Reset the calculator's memory (MEM).	
Adjust the contrast.	
Set the viewing window (domain and range).	
Graph a function by putting its formula into $Y_1 =$	
See values of a function in a Table; set the Table increment (TBLSET).	
Move around easily from Home screen to Graph screen to Table.	
Do basic linear functions with these calculator problems:	
1. Graph all three together on the calculator and tell what I see: $Y_1 = 2x - 3 \quad Y_2 = 2x + 1 \quad Y_3 = 2x + 5$	
2. Graph all three together on the calculator and tell what I see: $Y_1 = (\frac{1}{2})x + 2 \quad Y_2 = 0.875x + 2 \quad Y_3 = 3x + 2$	
Use a calculator to explore a linear situation:	
1. Baby Kalusha at two weeks old weighed 7 pounds and at four weeks old weighs 8 pounds. Assume baby Kalusha's weight gain per week will be constant (stay the same) for her first ten weeks of life. Find a function that gives Kalusha's weight as a function of time.	
2. Use the calculator to display a graph of the function.	
3. Use the Table feature to find Kalusha's weight at birth and at ten weeks.	

5 Understanding Slope and Rate of Change

Slope in the Real World

Slant, tilt, incline, pitch, grade—these are just a few of the words commonly used as synonyms for *slope* in everyday speech. In the real world, slope is most significant due to gravity. The human body is finely tuned to recognize the two slope benchmarks: horizontal and vertical. We can stand still only when our weight is precisely distributed vertically over our feet. When walking along a horizontal path, we quickly notice that even a slight uphill grade takes additional energy for us to keep walking at the same rate.

All our modes of transportation are designed to cope with slope. Bicycles have gears that can be adjusted for slopes of different steepness. Autos and trucks have powerful engines, brakes, transmissions, and other features such as four-wheel drive in order to ascend and descend slopes quickly and safely.

Quantifying Slope

Level, steep, gradual, flat, sheer, ascending, descending—these adjectives are used in everyday speech to describe the amount of slope. But carpenters, pilots, landscapers, surveyors, architects, road builders, and other people who work with slopes on a daily basis need to be more precise. To describe slopes with precision, several methods have been devised for assigning a numerical measure to a slope. These methods fall into two categories:

▮ *Method 1: Slope measured as degrees from horizontal* Degree measures of slopes can range from 0 degrees (corresponding to horizontal) to 90 degrees (corresponding to vertical).

▮ *Method 2: Slope measured as a ratio of vertical rise per unit of horizontal run* Slope ratios are always given as vertical rise per unit of horizontal run (as opposed to run divided by rise) because this results in steeper slopes being assigned larger numbers. Slope ratios range from 0 (horizontal) up to infinite (vertical).

A slope angle of 45 degrees is the same as a slope ratio of 1 to 1 or 100 percent. The angle measure of a slope and its corresponding ratio measure are linked by the trigonometric function called *tangent*. The tangent of a slope angle is the slope's ratio.

Gravity exaggerates our perception of slope. Think of the steepest road you've ever driven up in a car. How steep was it? Many people think they might be able to drive up a 45-degree slope. But actually, for cars, a 5-degree slope is steep. Roads that descend at grades of 4 degrees or more usually have warning signs posted such as *7% Grade Ahead* so that drivers can be cautious and not overheat their brakes. A grade of 7 percent means that for every hundred feet of horizontal travel, the road will ascend (or descend) seven feet. A 7-percent grade corresponds to an angle of about 4 degrees. For cars, any slope more than 30 degrees is impossible. For walking, stairs become necessary when slopes get greater than about 25 degrees. Ramps for handicapped access are usually not allowed to exceed a slope of 5 degrees.

Slope in the Mathematical World

On a Cartesian coordinate system, the algebraic definition of the slope of a line joining two points is "the change in the *y*-coordinates divided by the change in *x*-coordinates." This definition is equivalent to the carpenters' definition of slope as "rise over run." The magnitude of a slope on a coordinate system is the same as slope in the real world if the *y*-axis is considered vertical, the *x*-axis is horizontal, and the two axes are calibrated in the same-sized units.

In Example 1, the line shown has a slope of $\frac{6}{4}$ or, equivalently, $\frac{3}{2}$. In fact, if we start on the line and move right 2 units and then up 3 units any number of times, we always get back to the line.

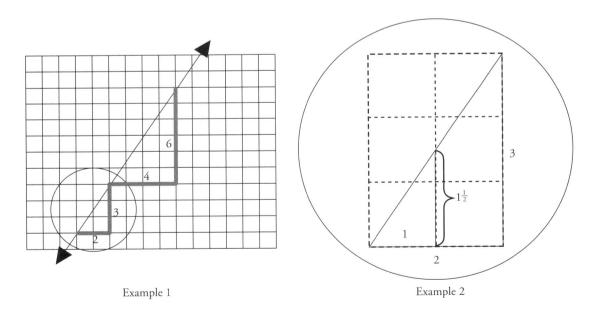

Example 1   Example 2

Example 2 shows an enlarged image of what's in the circle in Example 1. Notice that a slope of $\frac{3}{2}$ is the same as a vertical change of $1\frac{1}{2}$ or 1.5 units per unit of horizontal movement.

Why is the graph of $y = mx + b$ a straight line? Because the rate of change, *m*, per unit stays constant! To see this, think of how the graph would look if the slope changed at different points. Such a graph would have to look something like Example 3 or Example 4. In Example 3, for each move of 2 units to the right, the vertical jump gets larger. In Example 4, the curve bends smoothly; at point A the slope is about 1, and at point B the slope has increased to about 3.

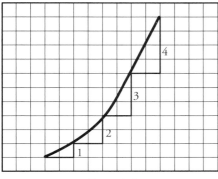

Example 3

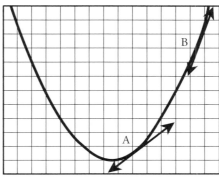

Example 4

Many introductory Algebra textbooks emphasize the *slope* interpretation for the *m* in $y = mx + b$. But far more useful is seeing *m* as the rate of change in *y*-value per unit of *x*-value.

Governments and industries use rates of change to forecast changes in population, revenue, school enrollments, and more. Forecasting changes depends on accurately figuring out the rates of change in past data. The mathematical field dealing with rates of change of functions is Calculus.

CHAPTER

6 Brain Research and Teaching Mathematics

Teaching is the art of changing the brain.
—*James E. Zull*

In *The Art of Changing the Brain,* James Zull (2002) describes recent discoveries about physical changes in the brain that occur when people learn. The lessons and suggested teaching approaches in *Active Algebra* are based on my personal teaching experiences, but they are also influenced in part by my interpretation of the ideas in Zull's book.

In the first part of *The Art of Changing the Brain,* Zull describes a natural learning cycle: experience—reflection—abstraction—active testing—experience—and so on, as the cycle repeats. Brain imaging studies show that each step of this learning cycle causes changes in a different part of the brain. In the latter part of his book, Zull discusses teaching approaches that are effective in motivating the learning cycle, and how those approaches change the brain. To get the whole picture, I encourage you to read Zull's book.

For math skills where the goal is automaticity, the traditional method of teaching has focused on "drill and practice." Brain imaging has shown that such learning creates bits of knowledge that exist in the *experience* part of the brain, but likely will not result in connections being made to other parts of the brain. As Zull explains:

> *. . . the actual process of calculating and getting answers is not a reflective activity. It uses the front cortex more than the back cortex. . . . It seems that calculation is more like a language activity, whose rules and pathways for action are already known. It is just application of those rules and pathways.*
>
> *But understanding the answer obtained by calculation and getting its meaning is more back-cortex focused. It requires reflection.*
>
> *With this in mind, a teacher might focus on making math more reflective. Calculating a right answer is important, but it does not generate understanding. To support learners in understanding the result of a calculation, we should challenge them to think about the answer, to recall things in their life that are related*

to that answer, and to examine where their answer puts things in relation to each other. (2002, 162)

The neural networks that hold knowledge of skills mastered by "drill and practice" are created in isolated parts of the brain. In order to understand the meaning and significance of these isolated factoids, the brain must create synaptic connections across the brain. These connections can't be made by more drill and practice, or by just telling students they exist. The only way students can make these higher-level connections is by personal reflection. When we focus the bulk of our students' time and energy on mastering specific mathematical procedures, we often shortchange the energy required for students to understand what they're learning.

So, what kinds of activities encourage reflection? It turns out that having students explain their thinking to others through speaking and writing is key. In Zull's words:

> *[To promote reflection we should require] learners to carefully assemble their plan for speaking. This plan must have specific content, and that content must be arranged in a way that accurately conveys the image that is in their brain. No clear image, no clear plan!*
> *But assembling the plan is how the image gets clear. (2002, 199)*

For these reasons, drill and practice is not emphasized in the *Active Algebra* lessons. Instead, the problems and tasks promote reflection by speaking and writing. Most problems are set in situations that students will find easy to talk about, such as restaurant tips, sale prices, a baby's weights, population data, and the distance traveled while walking or cycling.

Students are required to talk about mathematics in the *Active Algebra* lessons when they:

- **do mental math (students discuss their solution methods in their group before the answers are discussed as a whole class);**
- **make presentations (students write solutions before the presentation, which clarifies thinking and strengthens neural pathways); and**
- **create the end-of-unit project (students, working with partners, make a poster, which promotes a lively verbal discussion of math).**

The poster assignment (starting in *Active Algebra* Lesson 6) is especially designed for students to make higher-level connections in their brains. When students produce posters that include linear equations, functions, and tables and graphs all connected by a situation they've created, they must think of linear function representations as a whole, rather than as isolated pieces.

Including reflection in a math curriculum with the goal of teaching to promote understanding is not a new idea. What is new is the brain research that provides physical evidence to support this idea. We need to continually be on the watch for new brain research that may lead to even more effective teaching strategies.

From the Classroom: The Working Student Brain

Brain research can tell us a lot, but often I get the best insights into the workings of the student brain when I simply listen to my students. One Wednesday my sixth graders got into an argument. We were playing a "greatest game." First, I asked students to create a blank fraction sum:

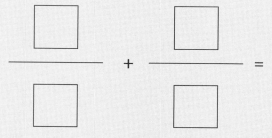

Then I drew four numbers from a set (2, 3, 4, 5, 6, 7, and 8) at random. After each drawing, the players wrote the number into one of the blanks of the fraction sum. Then they added the fractions. The player in each group with the greatest sum was the winner.

In one of the groups, Jackson had filled in the blanks and added them to get $4\frac{3}{4}$. Ellie had placed the numbers so her sum came to $4\frac{5}{6}$. They asked me who the winner was. I figured I'd been blessed with another "teachable moment," so I asked the class, "Which is greater: four and three-fourths or four and five-sixths?"

The class agreed that both fours were the same, so the question could be simplified to *Which is greater: $\frac{3}{4}$ or $\frac{5}{6}$?* Amazingly, a quick hand vote showed that the students were pretty much evenly divided between which was larger; a few stated that it was too close to call. I asked volunteers to come up to the board and argue their side of the answer.

Jackson told the class that $\frac{3}{4}$ was greater. He drew pies and cut them up. By his inaccurate sketch, $\frac{3}{4}$ actually looked greater than $\frac{5}{6}$.

Then Ali agreed with Jackson. She argued that since clearly fourths are larger than sixths, three of the fourths would be more than five of the "puny" sixths. I was starting to get worried.

Madelyn drew another pair of pies that made $\frac{5}{6}$ look slightly larger. I gave a silent cheer—the discussion finally seemed to be going my way. But then she said it was too close to call.

However, Annabelle argued that both $\frac{3}{4}$ and $\frac{5}{6}$ left only one piece of the pie remaining. And since the more accurate pie sketch clearly showed the fourth that was left to be bigger than the sixth that was left (things are going great so far, I'm thinking), but then this clearly showed that $\frac{3}{4}$ was more than $\frac{5}{6}$. I couldn't believe what I had heard! Was I going to have to step in and set things straight?

Then Livvy came to the board. She used a common denominator and stated that $\frac{5}{6}$ was greater than $\frac{3}{4}$ since $\frac{10}{12}$ was greater than $\frac{9}{12}$. I hoped her argument would stay in students' minds. So, I ended the class discussion and asked each group to discuss the question *Which is greater: $\frac{3}{4}$ or $\frac{5}{6}$?* Students needed to explain which, and why, in a group paper. (See Figure 6–1.) Of the eight groups, four felt that $\frac{5}{6}$ was larger, one group felt that $\frac{3}{4}$ was larger, and three felt it was too close to call.

The results of the group writing did not surprise me; student beliefs and opinions change just as slowly as anyone else's. What did surprise me was that not one group even remotely referred to the common denominator, 12, even though Livvy had shown this at the board.

During grades 4 and 5, these students had been drilled in how to find equivalent fractions. What happened? You might assume this was a remedial class, but it wasn't. In actuality, the thirty-four students in this class came from five different feeder schools and were not tracked. The rest of the day, I decided to pose the same question, *Which is greater: $\frac{3}{4}$ or $\frac{5}{6}$?*, to the rest of my classes. I received similar arguments and results in my other four sixth-grade math sections, and in my eighth-grade section as well! Based on my experience with my students that Wednesday, I decided to give them more concrete situations involving fractions to supplement the textbook's program of procedural skills.

(continued)

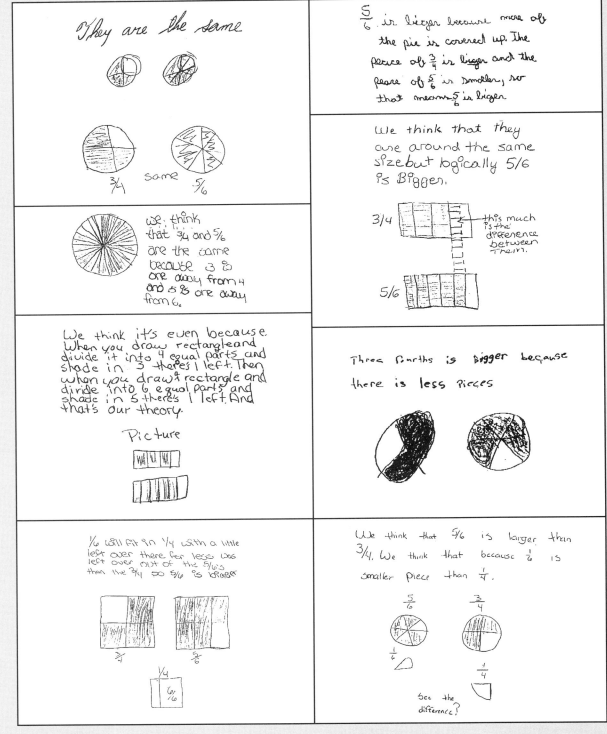

They are the same

3/4   same   5/6

$\frac{5}{6}$ is bigger because more of the pie is covered up. The peice of 3/4 is bigger and the peace of 5/6 is smaller, so that means 5/6 is bigger

We think that 3/4 and 5/6 are the same because 3 is one away from 4 and 5 is one away from 6.

We think that they are around the same size but logically 5/6 is bigger.

3/4   this much is the difference between them.

5/6

We think it's even because. When you draw rectangle and divide it into 4 equal parts and shade in 3 there's 1 left. Then when you draw a rectangle and divide into 6 equal parts and shade in 5 there's 1 left. And that's our theory.

Picture

Three fourths is bigger because there is less pieces

1/6 will fit in 1/4 with a little left over there for less was left over out of the 5/6's than the 3/4 so 5/6 is bigger

3/4   5/6

1/4   6/16

We think that 5/6 is larger than 3/4. We think that because $\frac{1}{6}$ is smaller piece than $\frac{1}{4}$.

$\frac{5}{6}$ $\frac{3}{4}$

$\frac{1}{6}$ $\frac{1}{4}$

See the difference?

Figure 6–1

Today, based on recent brain imaging studies, I believe I'm closer to understanding why the students had trouble with the question *Which is greater: $\frac{3}{4}$ or $\frac{5}{6}$?* Evidently, in their brains, the neural network created by "drill and practice" on common denominators was not connected to the network for comparing fractions. Eureka!

7 Mathematics Classroom Management and Discipline

As teachers, we need to prepare our students to become responsible, well-mannered members of society. Successful teachers have a plan that promotes and teaches positive social skills. Creating clear, consistent expectations for student behavior increases "time-on-task" and makes the classroom safe and less stressful for everyone. An ideal classroom discipline plan:

- **is simple enough for students to understand and remember;**
- **is easy for teachers to administer;**
- **results in a paper trail, including written student responses;**
- **is progressive (consequences for inappropriate behavior gradually escalate);**
- **has the approval and support of administrators; and**
- **is consistent within the math department and school.**

You may be fortunate to teach in a school that has a schoolwide approach to classroom discipline and provides a specific paper trail that supports the plan. Many schools, however, do not have such a plan, and hence this task is left completely up to the individual teacher. In either case, all teachers need to have a discipline plan specific to their classrooms and needs. The best way to devise your own plan is to discuss your personal plan with other teachers.

Student Dilemmas: A Case-by-Case Reflection

To stimulate discussion, here are eight dilemmas that require teacher action. Each of these dilemmas is based on a situation that I've had to deal with—at least once—in my teaching career.

For each of these dilemmas, ask yourself, *What would I do?* Discuss your answer with other teachers. On the pages that follow these eight situations, I reveal what I did for each situation.

Dilemma 1: Harassment

Eldon and Shirley sit near each other in the same group. Eldon leans his torso over Shirley's notebook and puts his elbows on her desk. He grabs her pen as she tries to work. Shirley tries to lean back to get away from him, but he persists.

What would you do?

Dilemma 2: Are you listening?

Ben is standing at the front of the class, presenting his group's solution. In the back of the room, Angela is talking to her friends; others are talking, too. I interrupt the presentation and ask Angela to stop talking and pay attention. Five minutes later, Angela begins talking again.

What would you do?

Dilemma 3: The defiant student

Arnold is wandering around the room, bothering other students during group work again. This is the third time in the past two weeks I've asked him to stay with his group and get to work. I've already kept him after class twice. I tell him to get back to his group, and again, to stay after class. After class he refuses to stay because he says he has to "go to a meeting with the football coach."

What would you do?

Dilemma 4: Out of control

Jana has been in my class long enough for me to know that she has a lot of personal problems at home. She is frequently angry and demands an extreme amount of attention. I've talked with her parents several times. They've told me that, yes, Jana is difficult to deal with and they don't know what to do about her behavior either. They claim she is out of control. Today, Jana won't sit in her seat. Instead, she tells me she's going to lie on the floor in the back of the room, which she proceeds to do.

What would you do?

Dilemma 5: The boyfriend breakup

Caryn, usually a great student, enters the classroom crying. I can hear her sobbing to her best friend Jackie, "He ruined my life!" I ask her what's wrong; her latest boyfriend has just dumped her. The whole class is distracted. Some are sympathetic; some are laughing.

What would you do?

Dilemma 6: The mystery student

Sid has never brought his notebook to class. Each day I give him a piece of paper to work on. Then I ask him to tape it in his notebook, which he must remember the next day. Sid is quiet and doesn't disturb other students, but he never does any of his work. I've called his parents twice and left messages. I've also mailed a letter to his parents, asking them to call me. They've never responded.

What would you do?

Dilemma 7: Cell phones

We have a schoolwide policy forbidding cell phone use during class. During group work, Calvin's phone rings. He takes it out of his pocket and whispers into it, thinking I won't notice.

What would you do?

Dilemma 8: Violence

I'm teaching in a portable classroom on the edge of campus. Though it's remote, teaching in a portable is a good deal because it has its own air conditioning system. However, ten minutes into first period a young man shows up in the classroom doorway. He is holding a knife in his hand. We have no other exit. He yells to Timmy, who is hunkered down in the back of the room: *Come outside or I'm going to come in and get you!*

What would you do?

From the Classroom: Student Dilemmas and Actions

Dilemma 1: Harassment

I walked over to Eldon. I told him to leave Shirley alone and keep to his own personal space. "But I'm not bothering her," he said. "Go ahead and ask her."

I sternly responded, "What you are doing can be construed as sexual harassment and I won't tolerate it in my classroom. Now get back into your own personal space and do some math. And stay after class and write."

After the bell I handed Eldon the Behavior Self-Evaluation form (see Reproducible F at the end of this chapter) on which I'd circled the positive behaviors *don't bother others* and *respect others' property*. First, Eldon wrote his answers to the two questions on the form (*Why is this behavior required of you?* and *How does your misbehavior affect others?*). Then we had a brief discussion, and he didn't bother Shirley again. Sometimes students do change their behavior when we tell them it is inappropriate.

Adolescents are often especially awkward in boy-girl relationships. Most schools now have a sexual harassment policy but leave it up to the teacher to figure out how to implement it in the classroom. As a teacher, I know I have the responsibility for protecting every student from sexual bullying. Unfortunately, adolescent girls are often the most reluctant to say *no* to boys; they may need your help. This situation was a minor incident, but it's best to be proactive. Later, when I saw Shirley outside of class, she thanked me.

Dilemma 2: Are you listening?

I told Angela to stop talking and stay after class and write. After class, Angela complained that her two friends were talking too; *why didn't I keep them after?*

"Oh," I said. "So you are ratting them out? I didn't happen to hear them. Tomorrow I'll tell them you told me they were talking too, and I'll keep them after class to write."

"That's okay, Mr. B., I'll write," Angela hastily replied. "No need to get my friends in trouble."

After the bell I gave Angela the Behavior Self-Evaluation form on which I'd circled the positive behavior *no talking while others are talking*. First, Angela wrote her answers to the two questions on the form (*Why is this behavior required of you?* and *How does your misbehavior affect others?*). Then I restated the fact that she needed to break this talking habit. She confessed that sometimes she just couldn't stop herself.

"Well, I'm here to help," I told her. "If you talk again during a presentation, you'll be here writing again. And if I have to get you to answer two more of these forms, I will have to involve your parents and the vice principal. I know when *you* make *your* presentation you'll want everyone to be respectful and pay attention."

Talking during a presentation may seem like a minor offense; I've visited classrooms where teachers let it slide by. But after a while, such talking becomes a bigger problem. We need to teach our students to be respectfully quiet in these situations; the other students have a right to listen and learn.

Dilemma 3: The defiant student

On Arnold's two prior "walkabouts," I had him fill out the Behavior Self-Evaluation form after class. Arnold's written answers to the form's two questions (*Why is this behavior required of you?* and *How does your misbehavior affect others?*) were proof that he knew what was expected. I had given him two chances.

Since Arnold didn't stay after class the third time, I considered it a defiance of authority. I made two copies of the earlier forms he filled out and stapled one copy of each form to a school referral form. On the referral form I checked *Defiance* and wrote *refused to stay after class, see attached*. I put the forms in the vice principal's box. Because the vice principal knows my system, I knew he'd back me up 100 percent by taking a higher level of disciplinary action (detaining Arnold or sending him to Saturday school).

(continued)

I also knew that the football coach wanted Arnold to be academically successful; the football meeting was a bogus excuse. Later at lunch I mentioned the incident to the coach, who said he'd talk to Arnold. Now I knew Arnold would be in for a stern lecture from his coach.

On the third offense of this kind, and whenever I send a school referral form, it's time to involve parents. I called Arnold's parents and left a message. Since I wasn't able to talk to them, I stapled the other copies of Arnold's Behavior Self-Evaluation forms to a letter to his parents (see Reproducible G at the end of this chapter), filled out the appropriate blanks on the letter, and mailed it.

Dilemma 4: Out of control

I realized that Jana's problems were too big for me to handle. I had already talked to her after class several times and didn't seem to be communicating with her. But I had twenty-nine other students in the room who needed to learn mathematics. I called the campus supervisor and asked him to come and pull Jana from class. He took her to the vice principal's office. I resumed teaching.

Later, during my preparation period, I filled out a school referral form and sent it to the school counselor. I knew the counselor was overwhelmed, but I didn't have the expertise to solve Jana's problems. My primary responsibility was to teach mathematics and maintain a positive classroom atmosphere in which learning could happen. I felt sorry for Jana, but sometimes teachers must recognize that some problems are truly out of their control.

Dilemma 5: The boyfriend breakup

I asked Caryn to sit outside of the classroom with her friend Jackie. I told them to talk it out, pull themselves together, and come back into class within ten minutes. Ten minutes later, Caryn and Jackie walked back into class, both with red eyes. I figured I might not get much math work out of them that period, but I was confident they would make it up. They were both great kids.

Dilemma 6: The mystery student

Because Sid wasn't bothering anyone, it could have been easy for me to simply let his behavior slide. But if he had continued to do no work, he not only would have failed to learn math, he also would have failed my class. I wanted all my students to learn, so I decided it was better to deal with Sid's problem immediately, before time ran out.

I pulled Sid aside after class and asked if he wanted to pass the class. "Sure," he mumbled.

"Well, then you will have to start working," I stated. "Do you know why your parents haven't called me?"

"They don't care," he shrugged. It suddenly dawned on me that Sid might not have the money to buy his own notebook.

"Tell you what," I said, "I have a bunch of notebooks that I got at an office supply store closeout last year. I'll give you one now. They cost ninety-nine cents and you can pay me sometime this semester whenever you get some cash. What color do you want?"

Sid took a black one. I continued to try to support Sid in class. Sometimes the quietest students are the ones who most need and deserve a teacher's attention.

Dilemma 7: Cell phones

I immediately asked Calvin to hand me his cell phone. I told him he could get it from the vice principal's office after school the next day. During lunch, I turned the cell phone over to the vice principal with a school referral form.

When a school comes up with a schoolwide discipline policy, every teacher must enforce the policy. If some teachers are lenient, it undermines everyone's authority. It's a mystery to me why teachers say something like *I know gum is forbidden by school rules, but I think it's a silly rule. So in my classes you can chew gum. Just don't stick it under the desks or tell the principal.* Such teachers may think students won't tell, but trust me—students frequently tell me about teachers who do this kind of thing.

All teachers eventually need the support of their colleagues. If you disagree with a school rule such as *no hats, no gum,* or *no mp3 players in class,* then you should argue for the rule to be changed. However, as long as it's a school rule, and until it's officially changed, you must enforce it to maintain the respect of your colleagues and your students.

Dilemma 8: Violence

"Put down that knife," I sternly told the young man standing at the classroom door. "Don't do something stupid that you will regret the rest of your life." (Later, when I thought about it, I figured I must have learned this by watching TV cop shows.) As I spoke, I picked up the room's phone and dialed 0 for the office.

"Las Pulgas High School," a student's voice cheerily came through from the other end of the phone.

I continued to look right at the young man, his knife at his side. "Get somebody down to my room now. This is an emergency. There is a man with a knife at my classroom door. This is Mr. B. in the portables, room 212." I spoke clearly—and tried to remain calm.

After three long minutes the principal and campus supervisor arrived. They had been summoned quickly via walkie-talkies. After a bit of serious coaxing, the young man decided to give up the knife and go with them to the office.

Later I found out that the young man's sister was in my class. He was angry with Timmy for something Timmy had done to her. I was lucky that nothing worse happened.

This situation was certainly one of my more frightening teaching experiences. Violence is not as uncommon in schools as people might think; some adolescents unfortunately have very short fuses. In a dangerous situation like this it is imperative to stay calm and rational despite any fear. Although such an incident may never happen to you, it is important that you think about what to do before it happens. If your school hasn't yet discussed what to do in the face of possible violence, by all means insist that you each have a plan that everyone knows about.

Classroom Management Forms

Three forms are available as reproducible templates at the end of this chapter: Classroom Expectations, Behavior Self-Evaluation, and Letter to Parents/Guardians.

Classroom Expectations

Classroom Expectations is a one-page form that I hand out and discuss with students during the third or fourth class meeting of the year. (I've found that if I give it out the first day, it just gets lost.) I also give a copy of the form to any students who later transfer into my class. Students tape it into the front of their notebooks.

Almost all teachers give out such forms; some schools require them. Some teachers require students to get the form signed by a parent or guardian and then return it. Personally, I don't require a parent's signature. The hassle of keeping track of the parents' signatures outweighs the benefits. I believe that classroom behavior is the student's responsibility, and I expect good behavior. If a student misbehaves, only then I will contact the parent for a discussion.

Behavior Self-Evaluation

Behavior Self-Evaluation is a form I use with students during class for citing minor infractions. The form lists all of the positive behaviors I expect of students. When students misbehave, I write their name and the date at the top of the form, circle the infraction (the positive behavior that's in jeopardy), and require that they stay after class to write their answers to the form's two questions, *Why is this behavior required of you?* and *How does your misbehavior affect others?* I don't hand out the form *during* class because it isn't fair to the other students to waste valuable math teaching time on a misbehaving student.

After the student finishes answering the form's questions, we briefly discuss their response. This whole process usually takes three or four minutes after class. There are two benefits to this process: first, the student has reflected on appropriate behavior, and second, I have a written document showing that the student is aware of my behavior expectations.

Once in a while I get a student who wants to make a big deal out of filling out the form: *You are wrong, I didn't do it! Shelly was the one talking, not me! You are mean! This isn't fair!* Some students even argue away most of their lunch period. I politely tell them to write their argument down on the form.

For persistent misbehavior (two or three incidents, two or three forms filled out, and no change in behavior), I make copies of the completed forms, staple them to a school referral form on which I write *see attached*, and send the packet on to the vice principal in charge of discipline. **Note:** It's helpful to keep twenty or so copies of this form at your desk, for instant access.

Letter to Parents/Guardians

Even though appropriate behavior is the student's responsibility, sometimes misbehavior persists. When a Behavior Self-Evaluation form has been completed consecutive times—and proven not effective—I phone parents to make sure they are informed and involved. Email is an alternative route to a phone call, but for me an email isn't as beneficial as a direct verbal discussion. Unfortunately, when I phone parents I'm often unable to talk to them and have to leave a voicemail (which—in the case of answering machines—may get erased if the student gets home before a parent!). Whenever I have to leave a message, I also send a Letter to Parents/Guardians. With this letter, I include copies of the students' completed Behavior Self-Evaluation forms. Usually parents respond by arranging to speak with me during the day, when we are both free.

Name _____   Date _____

Required Materials
- 9.75 × 7.5 composition notebook or spiral-bound notebook
- pencil and pen

All assignments, notes, and class work go in your notebook. Date each assignment. Tape your quizzes and exams into your notebook as they are returned to you. Bring your notebook, pencil, and pen to class each day.

Class Rules
1. Respect everyone and everything in the classroom by:
    - not talking while someone else is speaking;
    - working cooperatively and quietly with your group;
    - not using put-downs; and
    - using all materials with care.
2. Be on time and prepared for class. At the start of class, be ready with your pencil, pen, and notebook. Have all assignments completed. Plan ahead; during class time, you may only go to your locker or the restroom in emergency situations.
3. Food, drink, and gum are not allowed in the classroom during class time.

Positive Outcomes for Following Class Rules
If you follow class rules, you will likely:
- learn math;
- earn the respect of your teachers and peers;
- develop habits that are necessary for successful living outside of school; and
- discover that class is interesting—and even fun.

Negative Outcomes for Not Following Class Rules
If you do not follow class rules, you will likely:
- stay after class and respond to a Behavior Self-Evaluation form;
- sit alone outside of the classroom while I contact your parents;
- be sent to the vice principal's office;
- require a parent-teacher-student conference; and
- feel that class is boring and a hassle.

Grades
Your grade is determined by the percent of the points you earn out of the total points possible.

A   90–100%
B   80–89%
C   65–79%
D   55–64%

Attendance and Makeup Work
On the day of your return from an *excused* absence, it is your responsibility to make arrangements with the teacher to make up exams and get homework assignments checked off. Find out what you missed in class by looking on the assignment chart, asking another student, and then asking the teacher if you have questions. If you miss an exam and your absence is for only one day, you will be expected to take a makeup exam on the day that you return.

Name _____   Date _____

Positive Behaviors: Class Work

Whole Class

- Don't talk while others are talking.

- Raise your hand.

- Listen to directions.

Group Work

- Discuss quietly within your own group.

- Keep on task.

- No "mooching."

Individual Work

- Use time to work.

- Don't bother others.

- Talk quietly and only to those nearby.

- Don't talk during tests.

Positive Behaviors: General

- Don't leave class without permission.
- Use appropriate language.
- Respect others' property.
- Don't use cell phones/music players.

- Don't eat food or chew gum during class.
- Be courteous to others.
- Respect school property.

In your own words, write complete answers to these questions:

1. Why is this behavior required of you?

2. How does your misbehavior affect others?

Date: _____

Student: _____

Class: _____

Current Grade: _____

Dear Parent/Guardian:

Your student has recently had difficulty maintaining appropriate behavior in my class. I've attached a copy of my Behavior Self-Evaluation form that details the inappropriate behavior, along with your student's written response.

As a teacher, my job includes managing an orderly classroom atmosphere that supports the learning of all students. I know that as a parent/guardian, you also want your student to be successful. By making our expectations for behavior clear, we can help your student to do better in class, and also prepare him or her with the social skills he or she will need as an adult.

Would you please help me by discussing the attached self-evaluation with your student? Also, please let me know you received this letter by calling or emailing me:

Phone: _____

Email: _____

If you have any questions, comments, or suggestions, let me know a time and phone number when I can call you. I am available _____ .

Thanks again for your help.

Sincerely,

Mathematics Teacher

Linear Relations Lessons and Assessments

OVERVIEW

(continued)

OVERVIEW *CONTINUED*

Overview

Lessons 1 through 4 focus on understanding the general formula for linear relationships, $y = mx + b$. In Lesson 1 students work with in-out tables and relate the table values to the formula $y = mx + b$. They see that b is the starting value (y-value when x is 0) and m is the rate of increase in y per unit of x.

Skills

Working with $y = mx + b$

Positive rates of change

Mental Math Start-up

Figuring 5 percent, 10 percent, or 15 percent of a number

Core Problems

1.1 Baby Madelyn's Weight

1.2 Arnold's Savings

1.3 Solving Equations

1.4 Realistic Equations

Additional Problems

1.5 Baby Olivia's Weight

1.6 More Baby Data

1.7 More Equations

Mental Math Start-up

Figuring 5 Percent, 10 Percent, or 15 Percent of a Number

Note to the teacher: The mental math problems below are intended to be read aloud to students and need not be photocopied. Read each problem aloud twice, then allow students time to do the mental calculations and write down their answers. Then read the next problem. After all five problems have been read, put the problems up somewhere so students can see them, and give time for students to discuss the solutions. For more details, see Chapter 2, "Teaching Mental Math."

1. What is a 10% tip on a bill of $30?
2. Find a 10% tip on a bill of $65.
3. How much is a 5% service charge on $120?
4. What is a 15% tip on a bill of $80?
5. A 15% "late fee" is added on to a bill of $70. How much is the late fee?

Optional: More Mental Math

1. What is a 10% tip on a bill of $5?
2. Find a 5% delivery charge for a pizza costing $5.
3. Find a 15% "late fee" on a payment of $5.
4. How much is a 20% tip on a bill of $50?
5. At the Rich Rags store, employees get a 15% discount. How much is the discount on duds priced at $80?

Core Problems

1.1 Baby Madelyn's Weight

Little baby Madelyn weighed $6\frac{1}{2}$ pounds at birth and gained $\frac{1}{2}$ pound per week.

a. Make an in-out table showing Madelyn's weight for each of her first 10 weeks.

b. Find a formula that gives Madelyn's weight, y, in pounds as a function of her age, x, in weeks.

c. If the trend continues, how many weeks until Madelyn weighs 20 pounds?

1.2 Arnold's Savings

Arnold wants to have \$90 to buy his Mom's birthday present. He puts the same amount of money into a jar each evening. The table shows how much money is in the jar each evening for the first week.

x, Evening	0	1	2	3	4	5	6
y, \$ in Jar	\$9.00	\$9.75	\$10.50	\$11.25	\$12.00	\$12.75	\$13.50

a. Find a formula that tells how much money, y, is in the jar on evening x.

b. How much will Arnold have in his jar on evening 7? On evening 20? Discuss with a partner efficient ways to use a graphing calculator to get these answers. Be prepared to share at least one of your methods with the class.

c. How many weeks until there is \$90 in the jar?

   Note: To answer question c, you can find the value of x so that $75x + 9 = 90$.

Core Problems

1.3 Solving Equations

Example: Solve $3x + 5 = 17$.
Here is Arnold's logic:

Arnold thinks...	Arnold writes...
I'll copy the equation.	$3x + 5 = 17$
What number plus five gives seventeen? Twelve plus five is seventeen, so the $3x$ must equal 12.	$3x = 12$
What number times three gives twelve? Three times four is twelve, so x must be 4.	$x = 4$

Solve the following equations. Keep track of your thinking by writing down your steps like Arnold did.

a. $9x + 4 = 40$ **b.** $7x - 11 = 10$ **c.** $24 = 9 + 3x$ **d.** $16x - 3 = 5$

1.4 Realistic Equations

Realistic equations—from banking, chemistry, architecture, statistics, and so forth—often involve decimals and/or fractions.

Solve $7x + 2.6 = 11.7$.
Here is Berea's thinking:

Berea thinks...	Berea writes...
I'll copy the equation.	$7x + 2.6 = 11.7$
What number plus two point six gives eleven point seven? The number must be two point six less than eleven point seven. I'll get a calculator. Input 11.7 then subtract 2.6 gives 9.1.	$7x = 9.1$
What number times seven gives nine point one? I'll use a calculator to divide 9.1 by 7. I get 1.3. Seems like a weird answer. I'll check it. Input $7(1.3) + 2.6$ and press ENTER. I get 11.7. Yes! I'm right, as usual!	$x = 1.3$

Solve the following equations. Keep track of your thinking by writing down your steps like Berea did.

a. $524x + 87 = 349$ **b.** $.75x + 9 = 90$ **c.** $2.3 = 16x - 5.7$ **d.** $.25x - 1.4 = 0.6$

Additional Problems

1.5 Baby Olivia's Weight

Baby Olivia weighed 6 pounds at birth and gained $\frac{2}{3}$ pound per week.

  a. Make an in-out table showing Olivia's weight for each of her first 10 weeks.
  b. Find a formula that gives Olivia's weight, *y*, in pounds as a function of her age, *x*, in weeks.
  c. How many weeks until Olivia weighs 20 pounds?

1.6 More Baby Data

Data for three more babies is shown in the next table. Assume the rate of weight gain per week stays constant. Copy the table and fill in the missing blanks for each baby.

Age in weeks x	0	1	2	3	4	5	6	7	8	9	10	Extra information
Kalusha	7											Formula: $y = \frac{1}{2}x + 7$
Annie					10							Gains $\frac{1}{3}$ lb. per week
Imani					8			11				NO other information

  a. Which baby weighs the most at 10 weeks?
  b. Which baby has the fastest rate of growth?
  c. How long will it take until all three babies weigh more than 20 pounds?

1.7 More Equations

Solve the following equations. Keep track of your thinking by writing down your steps.

  a. $12x - 28 = 68$
  b. $24x + 43 = 49$
  c. $4.6x + 42.3 = 57.02$
  d. $1169 = 2155x - 555$

Overview

In Lesson 2, students work with linear relations having negative rates of change. As x-values increase, the y-values decrease at a constant rate.

Skills

More $y = mx + b$

Negative rates of change

Using $y = mx + b$ with real data

Mental Math Start-up

Solving one-step equations

Core Problems

2.1 Smallville's Population

2.2 Real Population Data

2.3 Knots

Additional Problems

2.4 Minneapolis

2.5 Baby Alfred's Weight

2.6 Auto Depreciation

2.7 Symbol Manipulation

2.8 Optional: Find Data on Your Own

Mental Math Start-up

Solving One-Step Equations

Note to the teacher: The mental math problems below are intended to be read aloud to students and need not be photocopied. Read each problem aloud twice, then allow students time to do the mental calculations and write down their answers. Then read the next problem. After all five problems have been read, put the problems up somewhere so students can see them, and give time for students to discuss the solutions. For more details, see Chapter 2, "Teaching Mental Math."

1. What is a 15% tip on a bill of $200?
2. If $3x = 15$, what is x?
3. If $x + 40 = 30$, find x.
4. If $24x = 6$, find x
5. If $x - 9 = 6$, find x.

Optional: *More Mental Math*

1. What is a 20% tip on a bill of $30?
2. Find a 15% check-cashing service charge for a check of $1200.
3. If $x + 8 = 12$, find x.
4. If $4x = 1$, find x.
5. If $\frac{x}{5} = 10$, find x.

Core Problems

2.1 Smallville's Population

The population of Smallville has been declining steadily. Here's the data for years 2000 to 2005:

x years past 2000	0	1	2	3	4	5	6
y population	1200	1120	1040	960	880	800	??

a. What is the average rate of change per year of Smallville's population from 2000 to 2005?
b. Figure out a formula for y as a function of x.
c. If the trend continues, what would Smallville's population be in 2006? 2007? 2010?
d. Display this function as a graph and table on a graphing calculator. Use the display to predict when Smallville's population might go down to zero.
e. Do you think the data for Smallville is real or made up? Why?

2.2 Real Population Data

Here is the population data for Mountain Lake, a real town in Minnesota:

Years past 2000	0	1	2	3	4	5	6
Population	2078	2062	2047	2034	2031	2008	??

Source: http://quickfacts.census.gov/qfd/states/27000lk.html

a. What is the average rate of change per year of Mountain Lake's population from 2000 to 2005? How did you calculate this rate?
b. Demographers sometimes use the "average rate of change per year" to predict populations in the future. With this method, what would the prediction be for Mountain Lake's population in 2006? 2007? 2010?
c. If y is the population and x is the years past 2000, write a formula for y as a function of x that approximates Mountain Lake's population data.
d. Display this function as a graph and/or table on a graphing calculator. Use the display to predict when, if ever, Mountain Lake's population might go to zero.

Core Problems

2.3 Knots

Fergus is amusing himself by tying knots in a rope. (Not drawn to scale.)

He ties one knot in the rope and then measures its length: 87 cm.

He's bored, so he keeps tying knots. When he has four identical knots tied in the rope its length is 75 cm.

a. How long will the rope be when it has 6 knots in it?
b. What was the original length of the rope with no knots?
c. If y is the length of the rope and x is the number of knots, write a formula for y as a function of x. What is the maximum value of x for which this formula will be valid?
d. Get a length of rope. Tie some identical knots (no overlapping knots) and collect length data. Use your data to write a formula that gives length in terms of number of knots.

Additional Problems

2.4 Minneapolis

Here is population data for Minneapolis, Minnesota:

Years past 2000	0	1	2	3	4	5	6
Population	382,324	380,137	376,926	375,822	373,708	372,811	??

Source: http://quickfacts.census.gov/qfd/states/27000lk.html

a. What is the average rate of change per year of Minneapolis's population from 2000 to 2005?

b. Using the "average rate of change per year," what will Minneapolis's population be in 2006? 2007? 2010?

c. If y is the population and x is the years past 2000, write a formula for y as a function of x that approximates Minneapolis's population data.

d. Display this function as a graph and/or table on a graphing calculator. Use the display to predict when, if ever, Minneapolis's population might be 20 percent less than what it was in 2000.

2.5 Baby Alfred's Weight

Here is weight data for weeks 3 to 7 of baby Alfred's life:

x = weeks old; y = weight in pounds

x	3	4	5	6	7
y	7.0	7.5	7.9	8.3	8.6

a. Draw a scatter plot.

b. Find the average rate of change over this time.

c. Estimate Alfred's birth weight.

d. Write a formula for a trend line.

e. Forecast when Alfred might weigh 18 pounds. You can use the formula to write an equation and then solve it.

Additional Problems

2.6 Auto Depreciation

Six years ago, Arnold bought a new Strato-Cruiser convertible car. Since then, its value has depreciated (decreased) at a constant rate of $1100 per year. The Strato-Cruiser is now worth $9900.

a. How much was the Strato-Cruiser worth when it was new?
b. Express the value of the Strato-Cruiser as a linear equation in slope intercept form.
c. If the constant rate of depreciation continues, how old will the Strato-Cruiser be when its value reaches $0?

2.7 Symbol Manipulation

Each formula below describes a particular situation. Do the following for each:
- *Simplify each formula into the form* $y = mx + b$.
- *Give the value of* y *when* x *is zero (y-intercept).*
- *Give the rate of change of* y *per unit of* x.

a. $y = 600(2 + x) + 2000 + 50x$ [y is the price of an antique car; x is the number of years since 1950]
b. $y = 9(6 - 0.4x)$ [y is the weight of Berea's dog; x is the number of months from now]
c. $y = 30(100 + 8x) + 40(50 - 8x)$ [y is the dollars in Berea's savings account; x is the number of months from now]
d. $y = 7(10 - 2x) + 3(210 - 2x)$ [y is the miles left to travel to get to Winnemucca; x is the number of hours traveled]

2.8 Optional: Find Data on Your Own

Find a town, county, or state for which the population has increased every year for the past five years. Use the data as in Core Problem 2.1 to predict the population five years from now.

Overview

Given the graph of a linear relationship, students learn how to find a $y = mx + b$ formula that fits the graph. They'll estimate the value of m by using two points on the graph and the value of b by looking for the y-intercept.

Skills

$y = mx + b$ when rate of change is a speed

Mental Math Start-up

Estimating sale prices when given the regular price and percent off

Core Problems

3.1 Walking Fifty Feet

3.2 Walking Again

3.3 You Walk

3.4 A Classic Race

Additional Problems

3.5 Leaky Tank

3.6 Baby Ali's Weight

3.7 Textbook Math

3.8 Running Three Hundred Feet

3.9 Solving Equations

Mental Math Start-up

Estimating Sale Prices When Given the Regular Price and Percent Off

Note to the teacher: The mental math problems below are intended to be read aloud to students and need not be photocopied. Read each problem aloud twice, then allow students time to do the mental calculations and write down their answers. Then read the next problem. After all five problems have been read, put the problems up somewhere so students can see them, and give time for students to discuss the solutions. For more details, see Chapter 2, "Teaching Mental Math."

1. What is a 20% tip on a bill of $15?

2. If $8x = 6$, what fraction does x equal?

3. Shoes: Regular price is $80. On sale for 20% off. What's the sale price?

4. Hat: Regular price is $30. On sale for 40% off. What's the sale price?

5. Video game: Regular price is $70. On sale for 30% off. What's the sale price?

Optional: More Mental Math

1. What is a 15% tip on a bill of $50?

2. If $3x = 63$, find x.

3. Coat: Regular price $30. On sale for 20% off. What's the sale price?

4. DVD reader: Regular price $110. On sale for 60% off. What's the sale price?

5. Concert tickets: Regular price $40. On sale for 15% off. What's the sale price?

Core Problems

3.1 Walking Fifty Feet

Arnold and Berea each walk a 50-foot path. The following graph shows how far each has gone at various times.

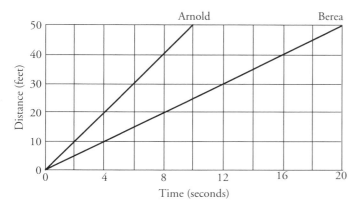

a. Who went faster?
b. How fast did each walk?
c. Find equations that give each person's distance from start as a function of time.
d. Suppose they keep on walking in a straight line past the 50-foot marker at the same rates. How far apart will they be after Arnold has gone 100 feet?

3.2 Walking Again

Arnold and Berea walk the 50-foot path again according to the next graph.

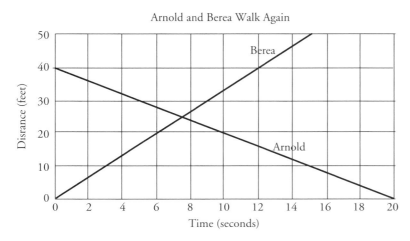

a. Describe in your own words what the graph tells about their movements.
b. Find an equation for each person.
c. When and where, if ever, will they meet?

Core Problems

3.3 You Walk

Walk a 50-foot path twice. Time how many seconds it takes in each case.

a. Start from 0 and *saunter* 50 feet at a constant speed.
b. Start at 50 feet out and *scurry* the 50 feet back at a constant speed.
c. Draw a graph for each case, both on the same set of axes.
d. How fast were you going in each case?

3.4 A Classic Race

A hare and tortoise are racing on a 48-foot path. Both travel at constant speeds. The hare travels at 3 feet per second. The hare knows the tortoise travels at 2 feet per second. The hare wants to make the race close, so she will give the tortoise a head start. How much of a head start should the hare give the tortoise so the hare wins by just a hair?

Additional Problems

3.5 Leaky Tank

Water is seeping out of a water tank. Each minute, the height of the water in the tank is measured in inches.

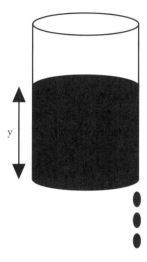

Here is the data for the first six minutes:

# minutes, x	0	1	2	3	4	5	6
height of water in tank (inches), y	50	46	42	38	34	30	26

Here is a graph of this situation:

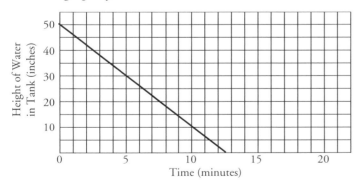

a. Find a formula for y in terms of x.

b. Find the exact value when the graph hits the x-axis.

c. Find the y-value when x is –5. Explain in your own words what these numbers mean in terms of height of water and time.

Additional Problems

3.6 Baby Ali's Weight

Baby Ali gains weight at a constant rate per week. After 4 weeks baby Ali weighs 10 pounds and after 8 weeks she weighs 11 pounds.

a. What is Ali's average weight gain per week?
b. How much did Ali weigh at birth?
c. Write a formula for Ali's weight in terms of her age in weeks.
d. How much did Ali weigh after 10 weeks?
e. When will Ali weigh 20 pounds?

3.7 Textbook Math

Answer the following questions. They're similar to those you'll find on standardized math tests.

a. Find the equation $y = mx + b$ of a line going through the points (4, 10) and (8, 11). Find the y-intercept.
b. Compare this problem with Additional Problem 3.6. How are they alike? Different?
c. Abstract Algebra: A line goes through points (4, 7) and (6, 12). Find the y-coordinate when the x-coordinate is 10.

3.8 Running Three Hundred Feet

Arnold and Berea jog along a 300-foot path according to the next graph.

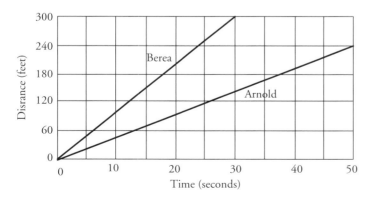

a. Who ran faster? How do you know?
b. Find an equation for each person.
c. If they keep on jogging, how long until they are 520 feet apart?

Additional Problems

3.9 Solving Equations

Solve the following equations. Keep track of your thinking by writing down your steps.

a. $10x + 40 = 55$

b. $19787553 = 78140x - 60007$

c. $4.3x + 7.5 = 35.02$

Quiz A

Mental Math

Assessing Lessons 1–3

Mental Math

These mental math problems should be read aloud to students sometime during the quiz. Use the same procedures as when mental math was done during the lessons. Read each problem only twice. Students write down the answers. You may want to make changes in the problems if your students are moving through the mental math problems at a slower pace.

1. What is a 10% tip on a bill of $8?
2. A 15% "late fee" is added on to a bill of $40. How much is the late fee?
3. If $x - 12 = 9$, find x.
4. If $3x = 18$, find x.

Assessing Lessons 1–3

Name_____ Date_____

Mental Math

Listen as your teacher reads the mental math problems. Write your answers here. Remember, paper-and-pen calculations are not allowed!

1. _____   2. _____   3. _____   4. _____

Problems

5. *When baby Zenaida the anteater was 4 weeks old she weighed 6 pounds and when she was 7 weeks old she weighed 8 pounds. Baby Zenaida gains the same amount of weight each week.*

a. Fill in the table with Zenaida's weight for each week.

Age (weeks)	0	1	2	3	4	5	6	7	8	9
Weight (pounds)										

b. If x is Zenaida's age in weeks and y is her weight in pounds, write a formula for y in terms of x.

6. *Solve the following equations.*

a. $8x - 9 = 47$ **b.** $4.8 + 3.4x = 20.1$

7. *Arnold and Berea start riding along an 8-mile bike path at the same time. The graph below shows their distances traveled for part of the path.*

a. After 15 minutes, how far apart were they?

b. When Arnold finishes the 8-mile ride, how long will he wait until Berea finishes?

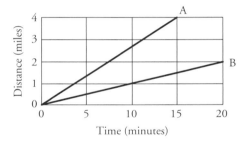

Lesson 4

Overview

Students continue finding linear formulas $y = mx + b$ given two points. Finding the intersection point for two linear equations is introduced in context and involves solving equations such as $84 - 40x = 100x - 16$. (The variable appears on both sides.)

Skills

Finding where two lines intersect

Mental Math Start-up

Figuring distance, rate, and time

Core Problems

4.1 Cats on Diets

4.2 Equations with Variable on Both Sides

Additional Problems

4.3 Populations

4.4 More Equations

4.5 Cricket Chirps

4.6 Abstract Math

Mental Math Start-up

Figuring Distance, Rate, and Time

Note to the teacher: The mental math problems below are intended to be read aloud to students and need not be photocopied. Read each problem aloud twice, then allow students time to do the mental calculations and write down their answers. Then read the next problem. After all five problems have been read, put the problems up somewhere so students can see them, and give time for students to discuss the solutions. For more details, see Chapter 2, "Teaching Mental Math."

1. What is a 20% tip on a bill of $210?

2. If $2x = 5$, what is the value of x?

3. Camera: Regular price $120. On sale for $\frac{1}{3}$ off. What's the sale price?

4. How long will it take to go 120 miles at an average speed of 40 mph?

5. How far will you go if you walk for 2 hours at a speed of 2.5 mph?

Optional: More Mental Math

1. What is 5% sales tax on a bill of $300?

2. If $x + 14 = 6$, find x.

3. Peanut butter: Regular price $3. On sale for 10% off. What's the sale price?

4. You bike for 3 hours, averaging 12 mph. How far did you travel?

5. You must walk 5 miles to Grandma's house at 2 mph. How long will it take?

Core Problems

4.1 Cats on Diets

Arnold has two cats, Archie and Shirley. The vet said Archie has to lose weight and Shirley has to gain weight. Arnold puts both cats on different diets. Here is the data so far:

Weeks on diet	0	3
Archie's weight (ounces)	240	222
Shirley's weight (ounces)	128	152

Assume each cat gains or loses weight at a constant rate.

  a. Find a formula that gives Archie's weight as a function of weeks on diet.
  b. Find a formula that gives Shirley's weight as a function of weeks on diet.
  c. Graph both formulas on a graphing calculator and estimate when the cats will both weigh the same. What will they both weigh then?

Core Problems

4.2 Equations with Variable on Both Sides

To answer 4.1c you could write an equation and use algebra. The equation you would solve looks like this example: Solve $7x + 8 = 3x + 20$. Here is Arnold's thinking and what he writes:

Arnold thinks...	Arnold writes...
I'll copy the equation.	$7x + 8 = 3x + 20$
I know that $7x$ is the same as $3x$ plus $4x$. So this equation is the same as $3x$ plus $4x$ plus eight equals $3x$ plus twenty. But aha! I can subtract $3x$ from each side of the equal sign. Therefore $4x$ plus eight equals twenty.	$4x + 8 = 20$
What number added to eight gives twenty? I know that twenty minus eight is twelve, so $4x$ has to be twelve.	$4x = 12$
What times four gives twelve? Is x equals three right? I'll check to see if it makes the original equation true. Does seven times three, plus eight, equal three times three, plus twenty? Yes, because twenty-one plus eight is twenty-nine and also nine plus twenty is twenty-nine.	$x = 3$

Solve the following equations. Keep track of your thinking by writing down your steps like Arnold did.

a. $7x - 2 = 3x + 10$
b. $3x - 11 = 4 - 2x$
c. $7x + 6 = 18 - 3x$
d. $84 - 40x = 100x - 16$
e. Now go back to problem 4.1c. Write an equation and solve it to find the week when the cats' weights are equal.

Additional Problems

4.3 Populations

Appletown is gaining population and Orangeville is losing population. Here is population data for these towns:

Years since 2000	0	5
Appletown population	3600	5750
Orangeville population	9600	8525

Assume the population of each town changes at a constant rate.

a. Find a formula that gives Appletown's population as a function of years past 2000.

b. Find a formula that gives Orangeville's population as a function of years past 2000.

c. Graph both formulas on a graphing calculator and estimate when the towns will have the same population.

d. Find when the populations will be the same by writing an equation and solving it. What will the populations be then?

4.4 More Equations

Solve the following equations. Keep track of your thinking by writing down your steps.

a. $16x + 8 = 6x + 134$

b. $6x - 21 = 15 - 10x$

c. $2.3x + 24.8 = 6.5x + 3.8$

d. $3600x + 5230 = 40750x - 2120$

4.5 Cricket Chirps

Biologists have found that the number of chirps, y, that some crickets make per minute is linearly related to the Fahrenheit temperature in degrees, x. At 68 degrees the crickets chirp about 124 times per minute, while at 80 degrees they chirp about 172 times per minute. What is the highest temperature, less than 68 degrees, at which a cricket will not chirp?

4.6 Abstract Math

A line goes through the points A at (4, 5) and B at (8, 7). Another point C on this line has an x-coordinate equal to 50. What is the y-coordinate of point C?

Overview

Lessons 5, 6, and 7 focus on slope, how slope is measured, and the connection between slope and rate of change for linear relations. In Lesson 5, the ratio measure for slopes is introduced. Students use graphing calculators to explore the relationship between slope ratio numbers and the steepness of a line on a graph. (See Chapter 5, "Understanding Slope and Rate of Change," for more insights.)

Skills

Measuring slopes with ratios

Slopes of linear graphs

Mental Math Start-up

Practicing percents and one-step equations, estimating sale prices, and figuring distance, rate, and time

Core Problems

5.1 Slope and Speed

5.2 Slope as a Ratio

5.3 Lines for Designs

Additional Problems

5.4 Alphas Eat Betas

5.5 Make a Square

Mental Math Start-up

Practicing Percents and One-Step Equations, Estimating Sale Prices, and Figuring Distance, Rate, and Time

Note to the teacher: The mental math problems below are intended to be read aloud to students and need not be photocopied. Read each problem aloud twice, then allow students time to do the mental calculations and write down their answers. Then read the next problem. After all five problems have been read, put the problems up somewhere so students can see them, and give time for students to discuss the solutions. For more details, see Chapter 2, "Teaching Mental Math."

1. What is a 15% tip on a bill of $8?

2. iPod: Regular price $300. On sale for 20% off. What's the sale price?

3. Sunglasses: Regular price $160. On sale for $\frac{1}{4}$ off. What's the sale price?

4. What is the value of x if $4x = 0$?

5. If you ride your bike 4 miles in 20 minutes, what was your speed in miles per hour?

Optional: More Mental Math

1. What is a 20% tip on a bill of $40?

2. Earphones: Regular price $70. On sale for 20% off. What's the sale price?

3. What is the value of $30 - 4x$ when x is 7?

4. What value of x will make $15 - 3x$ equal 0?

5. If you ride your bike 4 miles in 15 minutes, what was your speed in miles per hour?

Core Problems

5.1 Slope and Speed

Sampson walks a 50-foot path according to the graph:

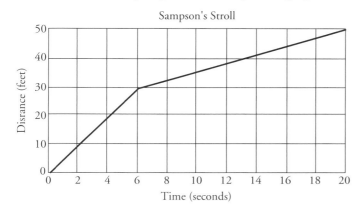

Sampson's Stroll

a. Was Sampson walking faster at the beginning of the walk or at the end? How does looking at the slope of the segments help you know?

b. What was Sampson's speed during the first 6 seconds? During the last 14 seconds?

c. What was Sampson's average speed for the walk?

Core Problems

5.2 Slope as a Ratio

Slope (slant, tilt, incline, pitch) is an important idea for graphs because it lets us visually compare rates of change. In addition, carpenters, pilots, landscapers, surveyors, architects, road builders, truck drivers, and other people work with and measure slopes on a daily basis. The steepness of a slope is usually measured by a ratio (the ratio of vertical rise per unit of horizontal run). When the x- and y-axis of a graph are in the same units, slopes are portrayed accurately. On a graph, lines that rise going from left to right are positive; those that fall are negative. Here are three examples:

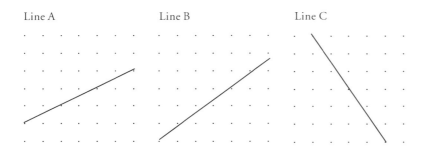

Line A   Line B   Line C

Slope $\frac{3}{6} = \frac{1}{2} = 0.5 = 50\%$ Slope $\frac{3}{4} = 0.75 = 75\%$ Slope $-\frac{6}{4} = -\frac{3}{2} = -1.5 = -150\%$

Write the slope of each of these lines as a fraction, decimal, and percent:

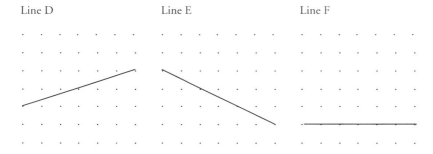

Line D   Line E   Line F

Core Problems

5.3 Lines for Designs

Try to reproduce each of the following designs in your graphing calculator window. For each design, write down the equation(s) you used.

Design 1

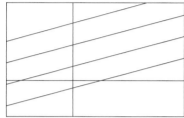

Four equally spaced parallel lines

Design 2

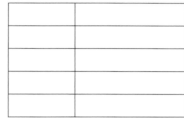

Four equally spaced horizontal lines

Design 3

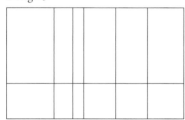

Four lines that appear vertical

Design 4

Four equally spaced parallel lines

Design 5

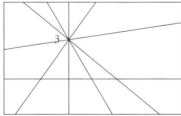

Four lines intersecting at (0, 3)

Design 6

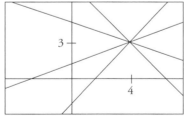

Four lines intersecting at (4, 3)

Design 7

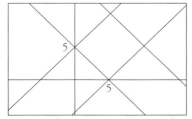

Lines form a square with two of
the vertices at (5, 0) and (0, 5)

Design 8

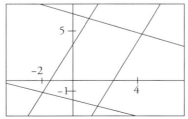

A parallelogram with opposite
vertices at (–2, –1) and (4, 5)

Additional Problems

5.4 Alphas Eat Betas

Berea has a big fish tank with two kinds of fish: Alphas and Betas. The first week there are 37 Alphas and 180 Betas. The Alphas are increasing at a rate of 3 fish per week and the Betas are decreasing at a rate of 2.5 fish per week (they're being eaten by the Alphas!).

a. If this trend continues, how many weeks will it be until the number of Alphas exceeds the number of Betas?

b. When there are no more Betas, how many Alphas will there be?

5.5 Make a Square

Find the equation for four lines that intersect to form a square with vertices at A(1, 2), B(4, 1), C(2, 5), D(5, 4). Keep track of your thinking by writing down your steps.

Overview

Students explore the two main ways slope is measured:

1. by angle from horizontal; and

2. by ratio of vertical rise per unit of horizontal run.

Also included in this lesson is an introduction to the end-of-unit project—a Linear Equation Poster—that will be planned by the end of Lesson 8, worked on in class during Lesson 9, and turned in at the end of Lesson 9.

Skills

Slope in the real world

Mental Math Start-up

More practice with percents and one-step equations, estimating sale prices, and figuring distance, rate, and time

Core Problems

6.1 Slopes Measured by Degrees

6.2 Slopes of Roofs

6.3 Ski Slopes

End-of-Unit Project

An Introduction to Your Linear Equation Poster

Additional Problems

6.4 More Real Slopes

6.5 Ratios from Angles

6.6 Handicapped Access Ramps

6.7 Do Slopes Have Length?

6.8 Optional: Tangents

Mental Math Start-up

More Practice with Percents and One-Step Equations, Estimating Sale Prices, and Figuring Distance, Rate, and Time

Note to the teacher: The mental math problems below are intended to be read aloud to students and need not be photocopied. Read each problem aloud twice, then allow students time to do the mental calculations and write down their answers. Then read the next problem. After all five problems have been read, put the problems up somewhere so students can see them, and give time for students to discuss the solutions. For more details, see Chapter 2, "Teaching Mental Math."

1. What percent is a $3 tip on a bill of $20?

2. Karaoke software: Regular price $44. On sale for 80% off. What's the sale price?

3. Sweater: Regular price $60. On sale for 30% off. What's the sale price?

4. If $x - 9 = 12$, what is x?

5. How fast are you going in mph if you run 5 miles in 30 minutes?

Optional: More Mental Math

1. What is 10% sales tax on a bill of $6,000?

2. If $x - 15 = 6$, find x.

3. Salsa: Regular price $3.99. On sale for 20% off. Estimate the sale price.

4. A ball travels 72 feet in 9 seconds. How fast did it go in feet per second?

5. You bike 45 miles at 15 mph. How long did it take?

Core Problems

6.1 Slopes Measured by Degrees

Slope is measured by the ratio of vertical change per unit of horizontal run. In the real world, slope is also measured as the number of degrees from horizontal:

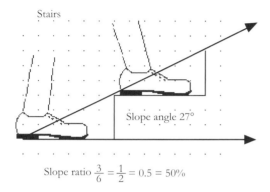

Stairs

Slope angle 27°

Slope ratio $\frac{3}{6} = \frac{1}{2} = 0.5 = 50\%$

In the stairs diagram, where would you put the protractor to measure the 27-degree angle? Degree measures of slopes can range from 0 degrees (horizontal) up to 90 degrees (vertical).

6.2 Slopes of Roofs

Slopes of roofs are often given as "5 in 8," which means that for every eight feet of horizontal run, the roof rises five feet vertically. Some standard slopes for roofs are:

a. 1 in 3 (slope $\frac{1}{3}$)
b. 5 in 12
c. 3 in 4

Accurately draw lines with each of these slopes. Then use a protractor to measure each slope angle.

6.3 Ski Slopes

The steepness of ski trails is usually designated by colors. Green slopes average about 10 degrees, blue slopes average about 25 degrees, black slopes average about 40 degrees, and double-blacks can average up to 60 degrees. Use a protractor to accurately draw lines with each of these slopes. Use a ruler to take the measurements you need and then calculate each slope ratio to the nearest whole percent.

End-of-Unit Project

A Linear Equation Poster will be due by the end of Lesson 9 as part of your assessment for this unit. You may work on the poster either alone or with one partner. (No more than two people may work on a poster.) For the poster, you will either make up a situation, or find real data, that leads to two linear equations.

Linear Equation Poster Specifications

Points	Poster must include...
3	*a statement of the situation* resulting in two linear equations (examples: cats on diets, town populations, saving and spending accounts, fish in an aquarium)
4	*a table* with at least two values for each equation
4	*correct equations* in $y = mx + b$ form
6	*a graph* showing both lines and their intersection
4	*an algebraic solution* for where the lines intersect
3	*a summary statement* (example: *Archie and Shirley will both weigh 14 pounds in 20 weeks*)
6	*quality craftsmanship:* sensible layout, no graffiti, originality

30   Total points possible

Deadlines

☐ By the end of Lesson 7, you should be prepared to tell your teacher whether you will work alone or with a partner and the situation your poster will be based on.

☐ By the end of Lesson 8, you should have preliminary data, equations, graphs, and calculations done. You must check with your teacher to get feedback on your preliminary work before you start your poster during Lesson 9.

☐ During Lesson 9, after your preliminary work has been checked, you will receive poster paper and will have most of the class time to complete your poster. Plan ahead: your poster is due at the end of Lesson 9's class. If you don't finish, you must come in during your free time to work.

Example A

An example of a successfully created student poster.

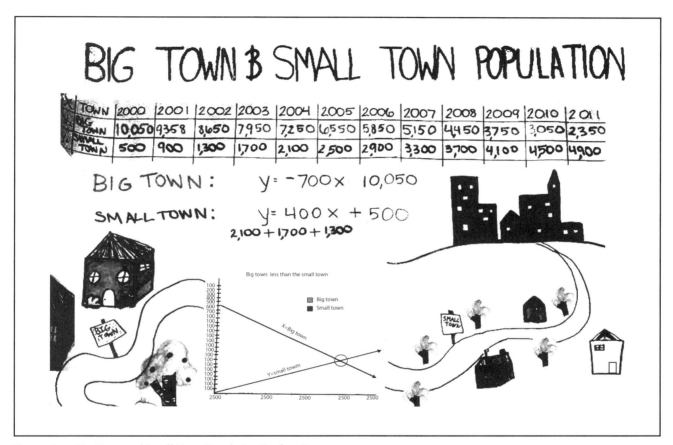

Figure 6-1   *Big Town and Small Town Population Student Poster*

Example B

An example of a successfully created student poster.

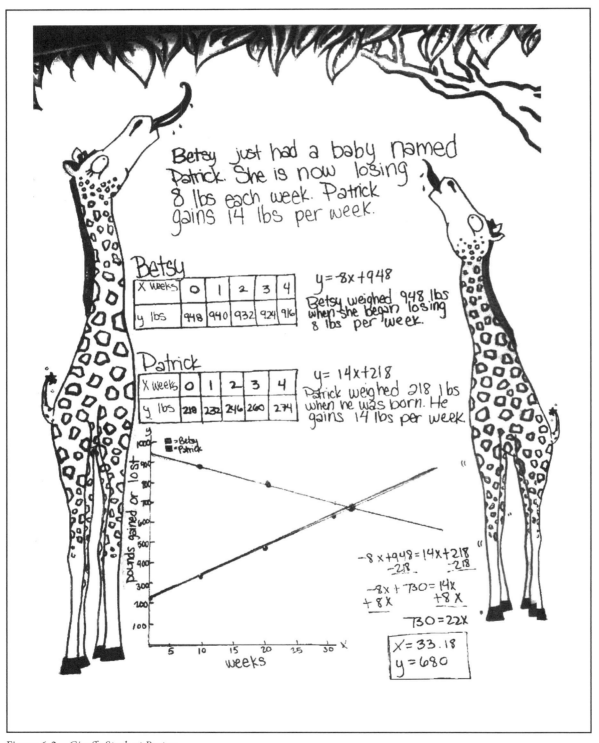

Figure 6-2 *Giraffe Student Poster*

Additional Problems

6.4 More Real Slopes

Accurately draw lines with each of these slopes. Use a protractor to measure each slope angle.

a. Roof 3 in 10
b. Road 9 percent grade
c. Skateboard ramp slope 1.5

6.5 Ratios from Angles

Accurately draw lines with each of these slopes. Use a ruler to take the measurements you need and then calculate each slope ratio to the nearest whole percent.

a. Line of ascent for airplane 25 degrees
b. Steepest hill on a rollercoaster 85 degrees

6.6 Handicapped Access Ramps

Building codes say that handicapped access ramps can have a slope ratio no greater than $\frac{1}{12}$. Which of these slopes would be okay? Why?

a. $\frac{3}{35}$
b. $\frac{4}{50}$
c. 20 degrees
d. 10 degrees

6.7 Do Slopes Have Length?

Arnold says: "Longer lines usually have steeper slopes."
Berea says: "The slope of a line doesn't depend on its length."
Who is right? Why do you think so?

6.8 Optional: Tangents

A slope angle and its corresponding slope ratio are linked by the trigonometric ratio called tangent. The tangent of a slope angle is the slope's ratio.

a. Pick at least seven of the slopes you drew in your class work and homework assignments. Make an in-out table with input as slope angle and output as the slope ratio (written as a percent). Put their values in the table.
b. Use a graphing calculator to check how closely the tangent of each slope angle agrees with each slope ratio in your table. (Caution: your calculator needs to be in degrees mode—not radians.)

Overview

In Lessons 5 and 6, students explored several real-world applications of slope and rate of change, as well as linear graphs using graphing calculators. Lesson 7 raises the level of abstraction of these ideas, including a note for students and problems that connect formula, graph, intercepts, and slope. Also, during Lesson 7, students begin to prepare for their Linear Equation Poster project, which will be completed in Lesson 9.

Skills

Connecting slope ratio and rate of change

Linearity in general

Mental Math Start-up

More practice with percents and one-step equations, estimating sale prices, and figuring distance, rate, and time

A Note About Slope, Rate of Change, and Linearity

Core Problems

7.1 Straights and Curves

7.2 One of These Things Is Not Like the Others

End-of-Unit Project

Linear Equation Poster Preparation

Additional Problems

7.3 Ordering Slopes

7.4 Which One Doesn't Belong?

Mental Math Start-up

More Practice with Percents and One-Step Equations, Estimating Sale Prices, and Figuring Distance, Rate, and Time

Note to the teacher: The mental math problems below are intended to be read aloud to students and need not be photocopied. Read each problem aloud twice, then allow students time to do the mental calculations and write down their answers. Then read the next problem. After all five problems have been read, put the problems up somewhere so students can see them, and give time for students to discuss the solutions. For more details, see Chapter 2, "Teaching Mental Math."

1. Arnold leaves a 20% tip on a bill of $50. How much is the tip?

2. New pillow: Regular price $40. On sale for 70% off. What's the sale price?

3. If $\frac{x}{6} = 30$, find x.

4. A watermelon takes 6 seconds to roll down a 120-foot hill. What is its average speed?

5. If $6x = 9$, find x.

Optional: More Mental Math

1. What is a 15% tip on a bill of $90?

2. If $8x = 1$, find x.

3. New tires: Regular price $250. Employee discount: 20% off. What's the sale price?

4. If $8x = 0$, find x.

5. An airliner flies 2400 miles averaging 600 mph. How much time did this take?

A Note About Slope, Rate of Change, and Linearity

You may realize by now that the value of m in $y = mx + b$ gives the rate of change of the y-values per unit of x. In the problems you have worked on so far, the units of m have been weight gain per week, population increase (or decrease) per year, dollars saved per month, and miles traveled per hour. But where does *slope* fit in?

Often scientists and mathematicians use the terms *slope* and *rate of change* to mean the same thing. Here's why: In Example 1 below, the line shown has a slope of $\frac{3}{2}$ or, equivalently, $\frac{6}{4}$. In fact, if we move right 2 units and then up 3 units any number of times, we always get back to the line.

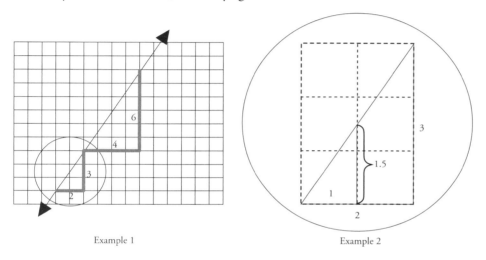

Example 1   Example 2

Example 2 above shows an enlarged image of what's in the circle in Example 1. Notice that a *slope* of $\frac{3}{2}$ is the same as a vertical change of $\frac{3}{2}$ or 1.5 units per unit of horizontal movement. For a straight line, the slope ratio is the rate of change!

Core Problems

7.1 Straights and Curves

Graph each of these functions on your graphing calculator. Draw a sketch of each graph's shape. If the graph appears to be a straight line, simplify the expression into $y = mx + b$ *form.*

a. $y = .05x^2$

b. $y = 2x + 3 - x$

c. $y = (3 - 2x)x$

d. $y = 47 + 3x - 53 - 3.5x$

7.2 One of These Things Is Not Like the Others

Example: Each row of the following chart lists an equation, a graph, a slope/rate of change, and intercepts information. Three out of four of these are correctly related. But for each row, one column does not belong.

	Equation	Graph	Slope	Intercepts
Sample Row	$y = x - 3$		Slope is 1.	x-intercept is 3. y-intercept is −3.

Look at the sample row. The graph of the equation $y = x - 3$ *should have a slope of 1, but does the graph shown have a slope of 1? No. The graph has a slope of −1. So either the equation or the graph is the "odd one out," but which one? In the third column, the slope given is 1, which matches correctly with the equation. So we suspect that the graph is the "odd one out." We can make a final check by looking at the Intercepts column. The x-intercept is given as 3, and the point (3, 0) fits the equation; the y-intercept is given as −3, and the point (0, −3) also fits the equation. Therefore, for this row, the Graph column is the one that doesn't belong.*

(continued)

Core Problems

7.2 One of These Things Is Not Like the Others, continued

Now it's your turn. For each row in the next table, find the column that doesn't belong, and explain why.

	Equation	Graph	Rate of Change	Intercepts
Row A	$y = 2x + 1$		Rate of change is 2.	x-intercept is −1. y-intercept is 2.
Row B	$2x + 3y = 6$		Rate of change is −2.	The intercepts are at (0, 2) and (3, 0).
Row C	$y = 4x$		Slope is 4.	The x- and y-intercepts are both at (0, 0).

End-of-Unit Project

Choosing Individual or Partner Work

By the end of Lesson 7's class, you need to have answered this question for creating your Linear Equation Poster:

☐ Will you be working alone or with a partner? If with a partner, who?

Choosing a Situation

By the end of Lesson 7's class, you need to have answered this question for creating your Linear Equation Poster:

☐ What situation will your poster be based on?

Additional Problems

7.3 Ordering Slopes

Arrange this list of slopes from least steep to steepest. Explain how you know your list is correct.

$\frac{7}{12}$ 45°   120%   .5   45%   3 in 5

7.4 Which One Doesn't Belong?

For each row below, find the column that's not like the others and explain why.

	Equation	Graph	Slope	Intercepts
Row D	$y = -3x + 2$		Slope is $-\frac{1}{3}$.	x-intercept is $\frac{2}{3}$ y-intercept is 2
Row E	$y = 1.5x - 3$		Slope is 1.5.	The intercepts are at $(0, -3)$ and $(2, 0)$.
Row F	$y = 0.5x - 3$		Slope is $\frac{1}{2}$.	The x-intercept is at $(5, 0)$ and the y-intercept is at $(0, -3)$.

Assessment Quiz B

Mental Math

Assessing Lessons 4–7

QUIZ B

Mental Math

These mental math problems should be read aloud to students sometime during the quiz. Use the same procedures as when mental math was done during the lessons. Read each problem only twice. Students write down the answers. You may want to make changes in the problems if your students are moving through the mental math problems at a slower pace.

1. Find a 20% tip on a bill of $25.
2. If $12x = 6$, find x.
3. Video game: Regular price $24. On sale for 50% off. What's the sale price?
4. Backpack: Regular price $40. On sale for 30% off. What's the sale price?

Assessing Lessons 4–7

Name_____ Date_____

Mental Math

Listen as your teacher reads the mental math problems. Write your answers here. Remember, paper-and-pen calculations are not allowed!

1. _____ 2. _____ 3. _____ 4. _____

Problems

5. *After Darling the Elephant gave birth to little Samson, she started losing weight and Sampson started gaining. Darling weighed 2,000 pounds at the start and Sampson weighed 800 pounds. After ten weeks, Darling weighed 1,820 pounds and Sampson weighed 1,240 pounds. Their weights continue to change at the same rates. How long until they weigh the same? Show the calculations you use to get your answer.*

6. *Write three equations that will make the design below on your graphing calculator.*

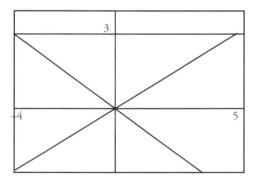

7. *The steepest road in town has a 20 percent grade. On the reverse side of this page, use a ruler to accurately sketch a road with a 20 percent slope. Use a protractor to measure the slope to the nearest degree.*

Overview

Lesson 8 consists of review problems and preparation for the poster workday of Lesson 9.

Skills

Review problems

Mental Math Start-up

More practice with percents and one-step equations, estimating sale prices, and figuring distance, rate, and time

Core Problems

8.1 Baby Jakey's Weight

8.2 Filling a Hot Tub

8.3 Calculator Designs

8.4 Solving Equations

End-of-Unit Project

Linear Equation Poster Preparation and Feedback

Additional Problems

8.5 Jerico

8.6 Turtle Race

8.7 Equation, Graph, Slope, Intercepts

Mental Math Start-up

More Practice with Percents and One-Step Equations, Estimating Sale Prices, and Figuring Distance, Rate, and Time

Note to the teacher: The mental math problems below are intended to be read aloud to students and need not be photocopied. Read each problem aloud twice, then allow students time to do the mental calculations and write down their answers. Then read the next problem. After all five problems have been read, put the problems up somewhere so students can see them, and give time for students to discuss the solutions. For more details, see Chapter 2, "Teaching Mental Math."

1. What is a 15% tip on a bill of $300?

2. Cellphone: Regular price $90. On sale for 85% off. What's the sale price?

3. Berea rides her bike 4 miles in 15 minutes. What's her speed in mph?

4. If $y = 6x - 24$, what is the y-intercept?

5. If $y = 6x - 24$, what is the x-intercept?

Optional: More Mental Math

1. What is a 20% tip on a bill of $5?

2. Guitar: Regular price $600. On sale for 5% off. What's the sale price?

3. It took Ranger Rick 20 minutes to run 4 miles. What was his average speed in mph?

4. If $y = 3x + 24$, what is the y-intercept?

5. If $y = 3x + 24$, what is the x-intercept?

Core Problems

8.1 Baby Jakey's Weight

When baby Jakey was 4 weeks old, he weighed 8 pounds. During the first 10 weeks of life he gained weight at a constant rate of $\frac{3}{4}$ pound per week. If the trend continues, predict Jakey's age in weeks when he will first weigh 20 pounds.

8.2 Filling a Hot Tub

Berea is filling up a cylindrical hot tub. She puts a hose in the tub and turns on the tap. After 10 minutes, the depth of the water in the tub is 6.5 inches. After 15 minutes, the water is 9 inches deep. The tub is full when the water reaches a depth of 22 inches. How long will it take to fill the hot tub?

8.3 Calculator Designs

Write four equations that will make each of the following designs on your graphing calculator screen.

Design 1

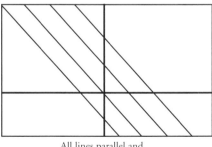

All lines parallel and
same distance apart.

Design 2

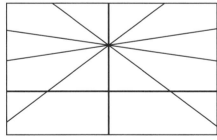

All lines intersect at (0,2)

8.4 Solving Equations

Solve the following equations. Keep track of your thinking by writing down your steps.

a. $7x - 4 = 59$

b. $14.5x + 24.8 = 58.15$

c. $101x - 1320 = 3720 - 179x$

End-of-Unit Project

Getting Organized and Getting Feedback

Prepare a prototype poster on an $8\frac{1}{2}$-by-11-inch sheet of paper by the end of the period, showing the layout for your poster. You'll need to include all the features described in the poster specifications in Lesson 6:

- ☐ a statement of situation;
- ☐ a table of values;
- ☐ a graph;
- ☐ equations in $y = mx + b$ form;
- ☐ an algebraic solution for intersection point; and
- ☐ a summary statement.

Have your teacher check your preliminary data, equations, graphs, and calculations by the end of the period. You must get feedback on your preliminary work before you start your poster during Lesson 9.

Additional Problems

8.5 Jerico

The city of Jerico is in an area of rapid population growth. Here is Jerico's data:

Year	1985	1995	2005
Population (Thousands)	239	281	318

   a. Find the average rate of increase per year of Jerico's population.
   b. Find an equation relating year and population.
   c. Use the equation to predict Jerico's population in 2010.

8.6 Turtle Race

Mary has three pet turtles that are great racers. In a race of D meters, turtle A beats turtle B by 12 meters. Turtle A beats turtle C by 15 meters, and turtle B beats turtle C by 5 meters. Assume each turtle moves at a constant speed. Find the length of the race (D).

Additional Problems

8.7 Equation, Graph, Slope, Intercepts

For each row in the next table, only one or two columns are filled in. Use the available information to fill in the answers that are missing.

	Equation	Graph	Slope	Intercepts
Row G	$y = 3x - 2$		Slope is _____.	x-intercept is _____. y-intercept is _____.
Row H			Slope is _____.	The intercepts are at (0,) and (, 0).
Row I			Slope is $-\frac{1}{2}$.	The x- and y-intercepts are both at (0, 0).

Overview

Lesson 9 is used for review problem presentations, poster work, and preparing a one-page unit summary. **Note:** Lesson 9 may require more than one class period if your period lengths are fewer than ninety minutes.

Skills

Connecting multiple representations of linear relations: table, graph, equation, and situation

Mental Math Start-up

More practice with percents and one-step equations, estimating sale prices, and figuring distance, rate, and time

End-of-Unit Project

Linear Equation Poster Completion

One-Page Unit Summary

Mental Math Start-up

More Practice with Percents and One-Step Equations, Estimating Sale Prices, and Figuring Distance, Rate, and Time

Note to the teacher: The mental math problems below are intended to be read aloud to students and need not be photocopied. Read each problem aloud twice, then allow students time to do the mental calculations and write down their answers. Then read the next problem. After all five problems have been read, put the problems up somewhere so students can see them, and give time for students to discuss the solutions. For more details, see Chapter 2, "Teaching Mental Math."

1. Estimate a 15% tip on a bill of $39.95.

2. Hamster: Regular price $20. On sale for 45% off. What's the sale price?

3. Arnold runs ½ mile in 5 minutes. What's his speed in mph?

4. If $y = 10x + 25$, what is the y-intercept?

5. If $y = 10x + 25$, what is the x-intercept?

Optional: More Mental Math

1. Estimate a 15% sales tax on a bill of $398.

2. If $y = 10x + 2$, what is the y-intercept?

3. If $2x = 1$, find x.

4. You bike for 20 minutes averaging 12 mph. How far did you travel?

5. A driver's test has 30 questions. You can get up to 20% wrong and still pass. How many correct answers do you need to pass?

End-of-Unit Project

Work Session

After you've cleared your prototype poster and preliminary calculations with the teacher, you will have the rest of Lesson 9's class to finish your Linear Equation Poster. The posters are due by the end of the lesson. The grading criteria for the poster are listed in Lesson 6.

One-Page Unit Summary

Look back through your work in Lessons 1 through 8. Prepare a one-page summary of the unit. You will be able to use this page during the in-class assessment (Lesson 10). Then you will hand it in as part of the assessment.

Make sure you include the following two items in your one-page summary:

- ☐ a brief description of what we have studied, in your own words; and
- ☐ specific ideas and/or skills you want to remember.

Overview

Lesson 10 is used to give students time to see each other's work, think about the quality of their own work, and show what they've learned and can do.

End-of-Unit Project

Linear Equation Poster Sharing
Linear Equation Poster Evaluation

Unit Assessment

The in-class unit assessment is the students' opportunity to show what they've learned. The assessment includes:

- five mental math problems;
- one slope problem involving a scale drawing with angle measurement;
- four problems about rates of change; and
- three equations to solve (two situations involving linear equations).

Linear Equation Poster Sharing
Linear Equation Poster Evaluation

End-of-Unit Project

Sharing Completed Posters

For the first half hour or so, you will be given about three minutes to share your completed poster with the class. In your presentation you need to:

- ☐ tell about the situation you used for your poster;
- ☐ point out the features of your graph;
- ☐ give the point of intersection; and
- ☐ state the meaning of the intersection point in terms of your situation.

Evaluating Posters

An important part of learning is reflection—thinking about what you did and how the worked turned out. How well do you think you did on the poster assignment?

After the posters are shared, you'll have an opportunity to do a self-evaluation by completing the Linear Equation Poster Evaluation. After you complete the form, you'll hand it in and your teacher will use it to grade your poster.

Linear Equation Poster Evaluation

Name(s)_____   Date_____

Now that your poster is done, it's time for you to reflect on the quality of your work. The table below lists the items required for your poster and the points possible for each (as given in Lesson 6).

In the Self-Assessment column, write the number of points you think you ought to receive for each item.

Your poster title_____

Poster must include . . .	Points Possible	Self-Assessment	Teacher's Assessment
Statement of the situation that results in two linear equations	3		
Table with at least two values for each equation	4		
Two equations in $y = mx + b$ form	4		
Graph showing both lines and their intersection	6		
Algebraic solution for where the lines intersect	4		
Summary statement (*Example: Archie and Shirley will both weigh 14 pounds in 20 weeks.*)	3		
Craftsmanship (originality, sensible layout, no graffiti, and so on.)	6		
Total points possible	30		

1. Comment on the overall quality of your poster.

2. Tell about one or more things you learned as a result of completing the poster.

3. If you were to do this assignment again, what would you do differently?

Mental Math

These mental math problems should be read aloud to students sometime during the unit assessment. Use the same procedures as when mental math was done during the lessons. Read each problem only twice. Students write down the answers. You may want to make changes in the problems if your students are moving through the mental math problems at a slower pace.

1. The Burger Barn bill was $60. How much is a 15 percent tip?

2. Coat: Regular price $30. On sale for 60 percent off. Sale price?

3. If $5x - 7 = 3$, what is x?

4. If you bike 4 miles in 15 minutes, what is your average speed in mph?

5. Which slope is steeper, 45 degrees or $\frac{2}{3}$?

Assessing Lessons 1–9, page 1 of 4

Name_____ Date_____

Mental Math

Listen as your teacher reads the mental math problems. Write your answers here. Remember, paper-and-pen calculations are not allowed!

1._____ 2._____ 3._____ 4._____ 5._____

Problems

6. *A skateboard ramp has a constant slope of 40%. Make a scale drawing of the slope and measure the slope angle to the nearest degree.*

7. *The gas tank of Berea's car is filled with 12 gallons of gasoline. After driving for 120 miles her tank has 8 gallons left.*

a. How many gallons of gas does Berea use per mile? _____

b. If y is the gallons left in the tank and x is miles she drove since the tank was full, find a formula that gives y in terms of x.

(continued)

Assessing Lessons 1–9, page 2 of 4

8. *Hereville is gaining population and Thereville is losing population.*

Years since 2000	0	7
Hereville population	4350	5246
Thereville population	9640	8205

Assume that the population of each town changes at a constant rate.

a. Find a formula that gives Hereville's population as a function of years past 2000.

b. Find a formula that gives Thereville's population as a function of years past 2000.

c. Find when the populations will be the same by writing an equation and solving it. What will the populations be then?

9. *Solve each equation. Write down your steps.*

a. $7x + 34 = 216$ **b.** $30x - 84 = 6x + 24$ **c.** $148.7 = 42.3 + 26.6x$

(continued)

Assessing Lessons 1–9, page 3 of 4

10. *Write four equations that give this design on your graphing calculator screen:*

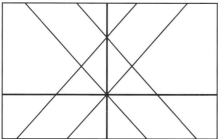

Two pairs of parallel lines. Lines intersect
at (0, 0) and at (0, 4).

11. *Look at the graph below.*

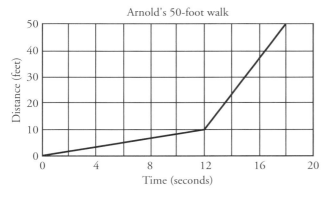

a. Find Arnold's speed for each segment.

b. What was Arnold's average speed for the 50-foot walk?

(continued)

12. *Water is leaking out of a cylindrical tank at a constant rate. Here is some of the data:*

Time (minutes)	4	14
Height of water (inches)	58	33

a. How many inches of water were in the tank at the start?

b. How many minutes from the start time will it take for the tank to empty?

13. *A line goes through the points (3, 21) and (7, 33). What is the y-coordinate of this line when the x-coordinate is 30?*

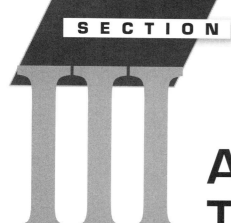

SECTION III

Answers and Teaching Insights

OVERVIEW

Mental Math Start-up

Mental math answers are not included. Instead, teachers are encouraged to figure out these answers mentally for themselves. When we do mental math along with our students, we understand better what is going on in our students' brains, and our own mental math abilities improve, too.

When discussing the solutions, encourage students to share their own methods as well as listen to your methods. Be patient and don't force your students to use a particular method even though it may be more efficient. Students will remember methods they understand far better than methods that are mastered only by rote.

From the Classroom: Mental Math

I was surprised that many of my students were unable to find 5 percent of a number using mental math. I asked the class if anyone knew an easy way.

Jackson said, "Just multiply mentally by five and then move the decimal two places to the left."

"Okay." I said. "But that's the same way you'd do it using paper and pencil or a calculator. Does anyone know an easier way?"

"I do!" answered Madelyn. "Just take ten percent, which is easy, and then use half the answer. That's five percent."

After a brief discussion about why Madelyn's method works, I had the students find 5 percent with a few more dollar amounts so they could practice what they'd heard.

Core Problems

Teaching Insight

Core Problems are designed to be appropriate for student presentation. See Chapter 3, "Teaching Using Student Presentations," for steps to teaching these using a system of student presentations.

1.1 Baby Madelyn's Weight

Students will need to count by halves. Birth is week 0.

a. The sequence of weights for little baby Madelyn for weeks 0 to 10 is $6\frac{1}{2}$, 7, $7\frac{1}{2}$, 8, $8\frac{1}{2}$, 9, $9\frac{1}{2}$, 10, $10\frac{1}{2}$, 11, $11\frac{1}{2}$.

b. A formula is $y = \frac{1}{2}x + 6\frac{1}{2}$.

c. To find the answer to part c, many students may continue sequence counting by halves until they get a weight greater than 20. Another method is to solve the equation $20 = \frac{1}{2}x + 6\frac{1}{2}$.

1.2 Arnold's Savings

This problem is similar to Core Problem 1.1, but with decimal values. The starting number is $9 and the rate of increase is $.75 per week.

a. A formula is $y = .75x + 9$.

b. To use a graphing calculator, put $Y_1 = .75X + 9$, then use Table to show the values.

c. Solve $90 = .75x + 9$ for x and get 108. So $90 will be in the jar after 108 days.

Some of my students don't solve an equation. Instead, they just use logic: "There is nine dollars to start, so we need eighty-one dollars more to make ninety dollars. Then eighty-one dollars divided by seventy-five cents gives one hundred and eight days." I point out that these are the same steps used to solve the equation!

1.3 Solving Equations

To solve equations, do your students use the traditional method or the show steps method? What are some advantages and disadvantages of each method?

Traditional Method	Show Steps Method
$3x + 5 = 17$	$3x + 5 = 17$
$3x = 12$	$-5 \quad -5$
$x = 4$	$3x = 12$
	$3x/3 = 12/3$
	$x = 4$

a. $x = 4$ **b.** $x = 3$ **c.** $x = 5$ **d.** $x = \frac{1}{2}$

1.4 Realistic Equations

Make calculators available to students to do this problem.

a. $x = .5$ **b.** $x = 108$ **c.** $x = .5$ **d.** $x = 8$

Additional Problems

Teaching Insight

Additional Problems are designed to be appropriate as homework or additional in-class work. Similar to the Core Problems, their answers can be presented through student presentations. See Chapter 3, "Teaching Using Student Presentations," for steps to teaching these using a system of student presentations.

1.5 Baby Olivia's Weight

This problem is similar to Core Problem 1.1, but students need to count by two-thirds. Once they get going they'll recognize a pattern. Birth corresponds to week 0.

a. The sequence of weights for the first ten weeks will include twelve entries:
$6, 6\frac{2}{3}, 7\frac{1}{3}, 8, 8\frac{2}{3}, 9\frac{1}{3}, 10, 10\frac{2}{3}, 11\frac{1}{3}, 12, 12\frac{2}{3}, 13\frac{1}{3}$.

b. A formula is $y = \frac{2}{3}x + 6$. Note that 6 is the starting weight and $\frac{2}{3}$ pound is the rate of increase per week.

c. To find the answer to part c, many students may continue sequence counting by $\frac{2}{3}$ until they get a weight greater than 20. Another method is to solve the equation $20 = \frac{2}{3}x + 6$.

1.6 More Baby Data

Filling in the chart for Kalusha and Annie is easy, but some of my students get stumped with Imani's chart. Her weight went from eight to eleven, which is a gain of three pounds in four weeks. Since the weight gain stays constant, she gained weight at a rate of three-fourths pound per week. Then count forward and backward by three-fourths to fill in the table.

a. Imani will weigh $12\frac{1}{2}$ pounds; Kalusha and Annie will each weigh 12 pounds.

b. Imani's rate of $\frac{3}{4}$ pound per week is greatest.

c. Since Annie is growing at the slowest rate, we need to find when she will be 20 pounds. We can either count by $\frac{1}{3}$ or solve the equation $20 = \frac{1}{3}x + 8\frac{2}{3}$. After 34 weeks Annie will weigh 20 pounds.

1.7 More Equations

a. $x = 8$ b. $x = .25$ c. $x = 3.2$ d. $x = .8$

2 Answers and Teaching Insights

Mental Math Start-up

Mental math answers are not included. Instead, teachers are encouraged to figure out these answers mentally for themselves. When we do mental math along with our students, we understand better what is going on in our students' brains, and our own mental math abilities improve, too.

When discussing the solutions, encourage students to share their own methods as well as listen to your methods. Be patient and don't force your students to use a particular method even though it may be more efficient. Students will remember methods they understand far better than methods that are mastered only by rote.

Teaching Insight

One-step equations are introduced in this mental math set. To solve these equations without paper and pencil, students must internalize two key equation-solving ideas:

1. addition and subtraction are inverse operations; and
2. multiplication and division are inverse operations.

From the Classroom: Mental Math

Students had trouble solving $x + 40 = 30$, but when I reminded them that x could be a negative number, they found the answer.

Students told me that in $24x = 6$, no number will work for x. I suggested, "What about a fraction?" Students gave me puzzled looks. I tried, "What can you divide twenty-four by to get six?" There was a resounding answer: "Four."

"Okay, then, dividing by four is the same as multiplying by what?" I inquired further.

After a bit, Annie volunteered, "One-fourth."

Good, I thought to myself, *x is one-fourth.* As I gazed around the class, I could see a few more faces that understood. I decided to give the class more mental math problems like this one so more students could grasp the concept.

Core Problems

Teaching Insights

Core Problems are designed to be appropriate for student presentation. See Chapter 3, "Teaching Using Student Presentations," for steps to teaching these using a system of student presentations.

In Core Problems 2.1d, 2.2d, and Additional Problem 2.4d, students are asked to use graphing calculators. If some of your students are unfamiliar with graphing calculator operation, consider taking a break from the lesson sequence and focus on the activity "Graphing Calculator Basics" in Chapter 4.

2.1 Smallville's Population

Smallville is a fictitious town with data made up so the rate of population decrease is constant.

a. Smallville's population is changing at a constant rate of –80 people per year. (The negative rate indicates that it is decreasing.)

b. Starting number: 1200, rate of change –80. So x years after 2000, the population is $y = -80x + 1200$.

c. $2006 \rightarrow 720$; $2007 \rightarrow 640$; $2010 \rightarrow 400$

d. Put $Y_1 = -80X + 1200$. Set the window to show the data: Xmin = 0, Xmax = 20, Ymin = 0, Ymax = 1500. Graph and then use Trace to follow the line down to where the y-value gets to zero. The x-value is near 15. (In this fake data it is exactly 15.)

e. Obviously the data is made up. It's highly unlikely that the rate of change would be exactly –80 for five years in a row in a real town.

2.2 Real Population Data

Remember, Mountain Lake is a real town and this is real data!

a. The rate of change does not stay constant over these years. But we can use the average rate of change. One way to find the average rate of change is to find the rates of change for each of the five years and then find their average. A quicker way is to find the total population change over the five years: 2008–2078 = –70 people. Then divide by 5: $-\frac{70}{5} = -14$ people per year.

b. In 2006 (year 6) we'd expect 14 fewer people than in 2005: 2008 – 14 = 1994 people; 2007: 1980 people; 2010: 1938 people.

c. Approximate population is $y = -14x + 2078$.

d. Zero population in 2148, if the trend continues.

Since each knot is tied the same way, the rope will shorten by the same amount for each knot. This is another example of a constant rate of change.

a. Since the rope shortened from 87 to 75 cm with three knots, the rate of change is –4 cm per knot. So the rope length after 6 knots will be $75 - 2(4) = 67$ cm.

b. The rope with no knots must be $87 + 4 = 91$ cm.

c. $y = -4x + 91$. Theoretically, about 22 knots could be tied (solving $-4x + 91 = 0$ gives $x = 22.75$), but this is probably not possible.

d. If you have groups do this, you could use ropes of different diameters.

Additional Problems

Teaching Insight

Additional Problems are designed to be appropriate as homework or additional in-class work. Similar to the Core Problems, their answers can be presented through student presentations. See Chapter 3, "Teaching Using Student Presentations," for steps to teaching these using a system of student presentations.

2.4 Minneapolis

Minneapolis also has seen its population decline.

a. Average rate of change has been $(372811 - 382324) \div 5 = -1902.6$ people per year.
b. 2006: 370908 people; 2007: 369006 people; 2010: 363298 people
c. $y = -1902.6x + 382324$
d. For 20 percent decrease, the population would have to be 80 percent of 382324, which equals 305859 people. Graphing will get us an estimate. Or we can solve the equation for x: $305859 = -1902.6x + 382324$, getting $x = 40.19$. So the population might be 20 percent less in 2040.

2.5 Baby Alfred's Weight

a. Students draw a scatter plot.
b. $(8.6 - 7.0) \div 4 = 0.4$ pounds per week.
c. Birth weight corresponds to $x = 0$, so an estimate is $7.0 - 3(.4) = 5.8$ pounds.
d. $y = 0.4x + 5.8$
e. One way is to solve $18 = 0.4x + 5.8$. You get $x = 30.5$. So if the trend in ÷ weight gain continues, Alfred might weight eighteen pounds sometime after thirty weeks. In reality, babies' weight gain stays nearly constant only during the first ten weeks of life, so this prediction likely will be inaccurate.

From the Classroom: Scatter Plots

In the student presentation for Additional Problem 2.5, the group's scatter plot had the y-axis scaled in units from 0 to 9. With this scaling, the points appeared to fall in an almost horizontal line all at the top of the graph. After the student presentation, I told students that they would see the pattern in the points better if the y-axis started at 6.5 and was calibrated in units of .5 (that is, 6.5, 7.0, 7.5, 8.0, 8.5, 9.0). I quickly redrew the scatter plot with the new y-axis calibrations. The new scatter plot showed the changes in the points better. Calibrating the axes to match the data is an important skill. That's why I never set up my students with a "precalibrated" scatter plot blank. I knew this would come up again, and each time they would get better at it.

2.6 Auto Depreciation

This problem deals with depreciation.

a. $9900 + 6(1100) = \$16,500$

b. $y = -1100x + 16500$, where y is the dollar value after x years from the purchase date.

c. Solve $0 = -1100x + 16500$ for x. Get $x = 15$, so if the rate of decrease remains constant, after 15 years the car will be worth nothing.

2.7 Symbol Manipulation

This problem provides a review of algebraic symbol manipulation. When put into the form $y = mx + b$, *the value of* m *is the rate of change and the value of* b *is the* y-intercept.

a. $y = 650x + 3200$; car's value at $x = 0$ (1950) was \$3200; gains \$650 per year.

b. $y = -3.6x + 54$; dog's weight at $x = 0$ (now) is 54 pounds; losing weight at a rate of 3.6 pounds per month.

c. $y = -80x + 5000$; money when $x = 0$ is \$5000; amount in the account is decreasing at a rate of \$80 per week.

d. $y = -20x + 700$; miles left to travel at start is 700; getting closer to Winnemucca at a rate of 20 miles per hour.

2.8 Optional: Find Data on Your Own

The website given in Additional Problem 2.4 is a good starting place. Consider having students write up their data and predictions, including a $y = mx + b$ *formula, as an extra credit assignment.*

Mental Math Start-up

Mental math answers are not included. Instead, teachers are encouraged to figure out these answers mentally for themselves. When we do mental math along with our students, we understand better what is going on in our students' brains, and our own mental math abilities improve, too.

When discussing the solutions, encourage students to share their own methods as well as listen to your methods. Be patient and don't force your students to use a particular method even though it may be more efficient. Students will remember methods they understand far better than methods that are mastered only by rote.

Teaching Insight

Mentally estimating the sale price of an item is introduced in this lesson. Finding sale price is a practical math skill that requires a comprehensive understanding of percent.

From the Classroom: Mental Math

For this mental math set, I asked students to share answers and methods within their groups. I circulated, listening to the discussions. Students commonly explained their method for finding sale prices like this: First find 20 percent of $80, the shoes' regular price. You get $16. That's the amount off. So then you subtract the $16 from $80 and get $64, which is the sale price.

In this method, the subtraction requires a calculated number to be remembered and often involves borrowing, which is challenging to do mentally.

I didn't hear anyone suggest the following shortcut method that eliminates the subtraction: *Since you get 20 percent off, you have to pay 80 percent. Therefore, the sale price is* $.8 \times \$80 = \$64$. *Done!*

During the whole-class discussion, no one suggested the shortcut method either. I decided to wait until Lesson 4 to tell the class about the shortcut. They might appreciate the shortcut method more after doing some additional sale-price problems the complex way.

Core Problems

Teaching Insight

Core Problems are designed to be appropriate for student presentation. See Chapter 3, "Teaching Using Student Presentations," for steps to teaching these using a system of student presentations.

3.1 Walking Fifty Feet

a. Arnold walked the path in 10 seconds, while Berea took 20 seconds. Hence Arnold walked faster.
b. Arnold: 5 feet/second; Berea: 2.5 feet/second
c. Arnold: $y = 5x$; Berea: $y = 2.5x$
d. It will take Arnold a total of 20 seconds to go 100 additional feet. After 20 seconds, Berea will go 50 additional feet. Hence they will be 50 feet apart.

3.2 Walking Again

In this problem, Arnold and Berea are going in opposite directions.

a. Answers may vary.
b. Arnold: $y = -2x + 40$; Berea: $y = 3.33x$
c. They'll meet after about 7.5 seconds at about 25 feet from Berea's starting point. (Answers may vary depending on estimates of rates of change.)

3.3 You Walk

Students should draw their individual graphs in their notebooks. For more about Core Problem 3.3, see "From the Classroom: Constant Rate of Change" in this section.

3.4 A Classic Race

If the hare gives the tortoise a 16-foot (or 8-second) head start, then the hare and tortoise will arrive at the finish at the same time. To be safe, the hare could give the tortoise a 15.9-foot lead (or a bit less than 16 feet or 8 seconds).

From the Classroom: Constant Rate of Change

I wanted my students to experience the correspondence between a constant rate of change and a straight-line graph, so I began Lesson 3 by having my students do some walking. We started with Core Problem 3.3.

Before class I used chalk to mark the start and end of a 50-foot path on the concrete walkway outside my classroom. We discussed what it means to walk at a constant rate: a smooth, even pace without speeding up or slowing down. I had my students time to the nearest second how long it took then to walk the path—the first time at a leisurely stroll (saunter), and then the second time at a quicker pace (scurry).

We returned to the classroom. I set up a graph on the board:

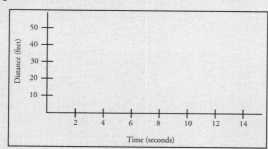

I asked Olivia how long it took her to walk the fifty feet at a saunter.

Olivia responded, "About fourteen seconds." On the graph at (14, 50) I placed a dot:

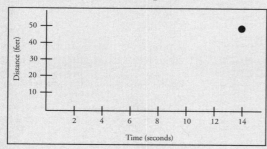

"Okay, now how far were you after seven seconds?" I inquired further.

Olivia thought for a second. "About halfway, twenty-five feet."

I placed another dot at (7, 25):

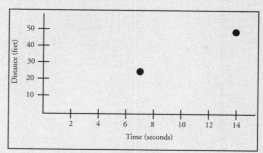

"How far had you gone after zero seconds?"

"Nowhere—zero feet!" Olivia declared.

"And for fifty feet, about how far did you travel each second?"

"Hmm," Olivia pondered. "I have to do dividing to get that. My calculator reads 3.57 feet."

"Let's put all that information on the graph. Also, since at every instant you were somewhere along the path, we can connect the dots with a straight line."

The graph on the board ended up looking like this:

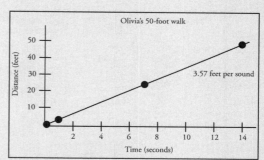

To conclude, I asked everyone to draw a similar graph for their data in their notebooks and also, on the same axis, to draw the graph for the faster pace.

Additional Problems

Teaching Insight

Additional Problems are designed to be appropriate as homework or additional in-class work. Similar to the Core Problems, their answers can be presented through student presentations. See Chapter 3, "Teaching Using Student Presentations," for steps to teaching these using a system of student presentations.

3.5 Leaky Tank

The situation, data, and graph are all given, which offers many ways to solve this one.

a. $y = -4x + 50$
b. Hits x-axis at $x = 12.5$
c. When $x = -5$, $y = 70$. Five seconds before we started taking measurements, the water height was 70 inches.

3.6 Baby Ali's Weight

a. $\frac{1}{4}$ pound per week
b. 9 pounds
c. $y = .25x + 9$
d. 11.25 pounds
e. If her weight gain stays constant, she will weigh 20 pounds after 44 weeks.

3.7 Textbook Math

a. y-intercept is 9.
b. Mathematically, this is the same problem as Additional Problem 3.6.
c. Different problem, same methods. Equation is $y = 2.5x - 3$. So when x is 10, y is 22.

3.8 Running Three Hundred Feet

a. Berea ran faster because her graph has a greater rate of change.
b. Berea: $y = 10x$; Arnold: $y = 4.8x$.
c. One way is to solve $10x - 4.8x = 520$, getting $x = 100$ seconds.

3.9 Solving Equations

A graphing calculator is recommended for b and c.

a. $x = 1.5$
b. $x = 254$
c. $x = 6.4$

Assessing Lessons 1–3

Mental Math

Mental math answers are not included. Instead, teachers are encouraged to figure out these answers mentally for themselves. When we do mental math along with our students, we understand better what is going on in our students' brains, and our own mental math abilities improve, too.

Problems

5.

a. Weights for baby Zenaida should be filled in with fractions as shown (or the decimal equivalents):

Age (weeks)	0	1	2	3	4	5	6	7	8	9
Weight (pounds)	$3\frac{1}{3}$	4	$4\frac{2}{3}$	$5\frac{1}{3}$	6	$6\frac{2}{3}$	$7\frac{1}{3}$	8	$8\frac{2}{3}$	$9\frac{1}{3}$

b. $y = (\frac{2}{3})x + 3\frac{1}{3}$

6. **a.** $x = 7$ **b.** $x = 4.5$

7.

a. After 15 minutes, Arnold had gone 4 miles and Berea had traveled 1.5 miles, so they were 2.5 miles apart.

b. Arnold will finish the 8-mile path in 30 minutes. But since Berea only travels 1 mile every 10 minutes, after 30 minutes, Berea will be at the 3-mile mark. If she continues at the same rate, it will take her 50 minutes to ride the next 5 miles. So Arnold will have to wait another 50 minutes for her to finish.

Mental Math Start-up

Mental math answers are not included. Instead, teachers are encouraged to figure out these answers mentally for themselves. When we do mental math along with our students, we understand better what is going on in our students' brains, and our own mental math abilities improve, too.

When discussing the solutions, encourage students to share their own methods as well as listen to your methods. Be patient and don't force your students to use a particular method even though it may be more efficient. Students will remember methods they understand far better than methods that are mastered only by rote.

Teaching Insight

Problems in science and math classes involving miles per hour and feet per second are often taught to students by using formulas and rote methods that emphasize memorization. To do this kind of problem mentally, students must raise their level of cognition and actually think of "mph" as the number of miles traveled in one hour. They must make sense of rate situations.

From the Classroom: Using Graphing Calculators

In class one day, while students were working in groups on Lesson 4, one group anxiously called me over. They were working on Core Problem 4.1, part c.

"Mr. B., nothing shows up on our graphing calculators!"

We use TI-83s in our class. The group had put the correct equations for the cats' weights into $Y_1 =$ and $Y_2 =$. But when they pressed Graph, a blank axis system appeared on the screen.

I tried to guide them. "You're doing okay so far, but in order to see the graphs you'll need to reset your Window ranges. Go ahead and press the Window button."

The students quickly followed my instructions, then looked at me, waiting for more answers.

"What are the units on your *x*-axis?" I asked.

"Weeks old," the students responded in chorus.

"And the smallest value for weeks is . . . ?"

"Zero!" the group shouted.

"So put *0* after Xmin = . Now what could you put in for Xmax = ?"

One student piped up, "The problem doesn't say! If we put in Xmax = 3, we won't see where they have the same weight. What are we supposed to do, guess?"

"Why yes! Guess!" I affirmed.

"But what if we're wrong?" Several students seemed to slump in their chairs.

"It won't break the calculator. Be adventurous! Guess, graph, then adjust. You'll also have to reset the Ymin = and Ymax = to show the weights." I enthusiastically left the group to work. I felt I had given them just enough information so they could figure out the rest for themselves. I think that students learn more when I don't give them too much information, but instead, "just enough."

Core Problems

Teaching Insight

Core Problems are designed to be appropriate for student presentation. See Chapter 3, "Teaching Using Student Presentations," for steps to teaching these using a system of student presentations.

4.1 Cats on Diets

Students need to find the parameters m *and* b *in* y = mx + b. *The value of* m *can be found by using the two points to find average rate of change. Archie is losing 6 pounds a week so his* m = –6; *Shirley is gaining 8 pounds per week so her* m = 8. *Their starter values are those given 0 weeks, which gives them respective values of* b.

  a. Archie: $y = -6x + 240$
  b. Shirley: $y = 8x + 128$
  c. After about 8 weeks they will both weigh about 192 pounds.

4.2 Equations with Variable on Both Sides

In this problem students get practice solving equations that start out with the variable on both sides. In the example, Arnold's thinking parallels the thinking students have been doing in the one-step mental math equations.

  a. $x = 3$
  b. $x = 3$
  c. $x = 1.2$
  d. $x = 6.25$
  e. Week 8

Additional Problems

Teaching Insight

Additional Problems are designed to be appropriate as homework or additional in-class work. Similar to the Core Problems, their answers can be presented through student presentations. See Chapter 3, "Teaching Using Student Presentations," for steps to teaching these using a system of student presentations.

4.3 Populations

a. Appletown rate of change: 430 people per year; $y = 430x + 3600$
b. Orangeville rate of change: –215 people per year; $y = -215x + 9600$
c. They intersect at (9.30, 7600). (When students use graphing calculators, you may have to help some of them with setting the Window range to see these functions.)
d. Solve $430x + 3600 = -215x + 9600$. If the trend continues, after a little more than 9 years the towns will have similar populations: about 7600.

4.4 More Equations

a. $x = 12.6$
b. $x = 2.25$
c. $x = 5$
d. $x = 0.1978\ldots$

4.5 Cricket Chirps

From the data points, the rate of chirping rises by 4 chirps per minute per degree. Since the cricket chirps at 124 chirps per minute at 68 degrees, $124 \div 4 = 31$ degrees. Then 31 degrees less than 68 degrees is 37 degrees. If the trend holds, the crickets would stop chirping when the temperature falls to 37 degrees. Another way to do this problem is to use the data points to find an equation that gives chirps as a function of temperature: $y = 4x - 148$. Solving for x when y = 0 gives x = 37 degrees.

4.6 Abstract Math

The equation is $y = \frac{1}{2}x + 3$. So when $x = 50$, $y = 28$.

5 Answers and Teaching Insights

Mental Math Start-up

Mental math answers are not included. Instead, teachers are encouraged to figure out these answers mentally for themselves. When we do mental math along with our students, we understand better what is going on in our students' brains, and our own mental math abilities improve, too.

When discussing the solutions, encourage students to share their own methods as well as listen to your methods. Be patient and don't force your students to use a particular method even though it may be more efficient. Students will remember methods they understand far better than methods that are mastered only by rote.

Teaching Insight

By Lesson 5, students have been introduced to these four types of mental math problems:

- ☐ Find 5 percent, 10 percent, 15 percent, and 20 percent of a number.
- ☐ Solve one-step equations.
- ☐ Estimate sale prices when given the regular price and percent off.
- ☐ Figure distance, rate, and time.

In Lessons 5 through 9, students practice more of these types of mental math problems to improve and strengthen their skills.

From the Classroom: Mental Math

It's been my experience that by Lesson 5 many students still aren't using the shortcut to find sale prices. I decided to pursue this further.

"Group 3, can someone in your group please tell me the sale price of the earphones?"

Imani volunteered her answer. "We got fifty-six dollars. I knew how to do twenty percent, just like doing the tip. The regular price was seventy dollars, so ten percent would be seven dollars. Then twenty percent would be twice seven dollars, which gives fourteen dollars. Then the last step is to take the fourteen dollars away from the seventy dollars, which gives the sale price of fifty-six dollars."

"What was the hardest part for you in doing this problem mentally?"

Imani immediately had an answer. "Subtracting the fourteen from seventy in my head!"

"OK. Good. Does anyone have an easier way to get this answer?"

Jackson offered one. "We could use the way we talked about yesterday. Since the sale price is twenty percent off, that means we have to pay only eighty percent of the original price. Eight times seven is fifty-six dollars. Done!"

I sensed that a few more of my students now knew the shortcut and understood enough about percents to know why it works. I made a note to keep asking them more "sale price" mental math problems in the future.

Core Problems

Teaching Insights

Core Problems are designed to be appropriate for student presentation. See Chapter 3, "Teaching Using Student Presentations," for steps to teaching these using a system of student presentations.

In this lesson students relate slope and the rate of change of a linear function. You may be asking, "Aren't slope and rate of change the same?" If you think so, read Chapter 5, "Understanding Slope and Rate of Change."

Graphing calculators are used extensively in Lesson 5. If you haven't yet used graphing calculators with your class, consider taking a break from the lesson sequence and focus on the activity Graphing Calculator Basics discussed in Chapter 4.

5.1 Slope and Speed

a. Sampson was walking faster at the beginning because the slope of the first segment is steeper than the second segment. Therefore, the rate during the first segment is greater.
b. Sampson went 30 feet in the first 6 seconds, so his speed was 5 feet/second. In the last 14 seconds he went 20 feet, so his speed was 1.43 feet/second.
c. Sampson walked 50 feet in 20 seconds, so his average speed for the whole walk was 2.5 feet/second. Note that this is not the mean of the rates for each segment.

5.2 Slope as a Ratio

The first three segments are intended as examples. You may want to count out with students the horizontal and vertical lengths of the first line segment. Some will make the error of counting the dots rather than the lengths and get 7 and 4 instead of 6 and 3.

Line D: $\frac{2}{6} = \frac{1}{3} = .3333\ldots = 33\%$
Line E: $-\frac{3}{6} = -\frac{1}{2} = 2.5 = 250\%$
Line F: $\frac{0}{6} = 0 = 0\%$

5.3 Lines for Designs

Students need time to explore the eight designs. Trial and error using graphing calculators works best.

Design 1: A variety of answers are possible, but m-values must be the same positive value and b-values at equal intervals.
Design 2: m-values are all 0 and b-values at equal intervals.
Design 3: It is impossible to graph a vertical line such as $x = 5$ using the calculator's Y = feature. However, the key term here is *appear vertical*. There are several ways of doing this. The easiest way is to make the slope very steep, such as $y = 1000000x + 2$.

Design 4: *m*-values are all the same negative value and *b*-values are at equal intervals.

Design 5: Since the *y*-intercepts of all lines are at (0, 3), all *b*-values must be 3.

Design 6: This is the same graph as Design 5, but translated 4 units to the right. One solution is to graph $y = m(x - 4) + 3$ for various values of *m*.

Design 7: To make the square appear correct, the *x*- and *y*-axes must be calibrated in the same size units. To do this using TI calculators, first select under Zoom the choice ZStandard, then ZSquare. Then the equations $Y_1 = x - 5$; $Y_2 = x + 5$; $Y_3 = -x + 5$; $Y_4 = -x + 15$ will form the square.

Design 8: The four equations $Y_1 = p(x - 4) + 5$; $Y_2 = p(x + 2) - 1$; $Y_3 = q(x - 4) + 5$; $Y_4 = q(x + 2) - 1$ where $p > 0$ and $q < 0$ will form the parallelogram. The values $p = 4$ and $q = -0.5$ give a nice picture.

From the Classroom: Using Graphing Calculators

My students were busy working on Core Problem 5.3 using their graphing calculators. As I walked around the room, I noticed that Group 5 was frustrated.

"Mr. B.! We don't even know how to get started doing the first problem!" The group was trying to write equations to make this diagram:

Design 1

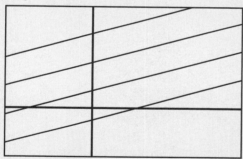

Four equally-spaced parallel lines

"Tell me what you see," I asked.

"Four lines!" The group gave a choral response.

"And what is special about these lines?" I inquired further.

"They're parallel?"

"So if they are parallel, what is true about their slopes?"

After a bit of thinking, the group recognized the similarity: "The slopes are all the same."

"OK, so make an estimate of the slope. Is it positive or negative?"

"Positive; it goes uphill from left to right."

"Correct. And is the slope more than one or less than one?"

"We don't know."

"Now remember, we measure slope as the change in the number of units of rise per one unit of run. So a slope of one means that for every horizontal move of one unit, the graph would rise one unit. Let's see you put your arms at a slope of one."

The students held their arms at angles of about 45 degrees.

"OK, now look at the lines in the diagram. Is the slope more or less than your arm's slope?"

"Less!"

"So give me a number for a slope less than one."

"Half. Point five."

"OK, go ahead and try some equations that have *m* equal to .5 and see what you get."

I felt that was enough of a hint, and left to observe another group. After thinking about this interaction, I decided my students needed more work in estimating slopes based on benchmarks. I made a note to do more "show the slope with your arm" exercises with everyone the next time I had the whole class together.

Additional Problems

Teaching Insight

Additional Problems are designed to be appropriate as homework or additional in-class work. Similar to the Core Problems, their answers can be presented through student presentations. See Chapter 3, "Teaching Using Student Presentations," for steps to teaching these using a system of student presentations.

5.4 Alphas Eat Betas

Equations are Alphas $Y_1 = 3x + 37$; Betas $Y_2 = -2.5x + 180$.

a. Setting the two equations equal and solving gives $x = 26$. So if the trends continue at the same rate, at week 26 the numbers of fish will be the same: 115.

b. There will be no Betas left after 72 weeks. At that time there will be 253 Alphas with nothing left to eat.

5.5 Make a Square

This may be a difficult problem because it takes several calculations to get the four equations.

$Y_1 = 3x - 11$
$Y_2 = 3x - 1$
$Y_3 = -\frac{1}{3}x + 5\frac{2}{3}$
$Y_4 = -\frac{1}{3}x + 2\frac{1}{3}$

6 Answers and Teaching Insights

Mental Math Start-up

Mental math answers are not included. Instead, teachers are encouraged to figure out these answers mentally for themselves. When we do mental math along with our students, we understand better what is going on in our students' brains, and our own mental math abilities improve, too.

When discussing the solutions, encourage students to share their own methods as well as listen to your methods. Be patient and don't force your students to use a particular method even though it may be more efficient. Students will remember methods they understand far better than methods that are mastered only by rote.

Teaching Insight

To introduce today's Core Problems you could add this mental math problem to check what your students recall about slope: "Which is steeper, a line with slope three-fourths or a line with slope five-sixths?"

From the Classroom: Mental Math

By Lesson 6, my students are very familiar with the mental math routine. Some are exceptional at finding tips and solving one-step equations. However, sale-price problems are still difficult. Many students are not using the shortcut of first subtracting the sale percent from 100 percent and then multiplying to find the sale price. This is an important idea, so I decide to write the steps on the board. First I write a new problem with the relevant percents and ask students to come up with the answers mentally:

Shoes: Regular price $90. On sale for 30 percent off.
30 percent of $90 = ?
70 percent of $90 = ?

I then add to the board:

30 percent of $90 = $27 → the amount you don't pay
70 percent of $90 = $63 → the amount you do pay; the sale price

Shortcut: First take the sale percent away from 100 percent to get the percent you pay. Then multiply to find the amount you pay.

Core Problems

Teaching Insights

Core Problems are designed to be appropriate for student presentation. See Chapter 3, "Teaching Using Student Presentations," for steps to teaching these using a system of student presentations.

Students will need protractors and centimeter rulers to do the problems in this lesson.

6.1 Slopes Measured by Degrees

Don't assume that your students know how to use a protractor to measure angles. You may want to ask a student to demonstrate how to measure an angle for the class. Emphasize that an angle is an amount of turn. Its measure is the number of degrees of turn it takes to move one ray of the angle into the other.

6.2 Slopes of Roofs

These answers are to the nearest degree:

a. 1 in 3: 18 degrees
b. 5 in 12: 23 degrees
c. 3 in 4: 37 degrees

6.3 Ski Slopes

Here are the slope percentages, also known as the *grade*:

Green slopes: 10 degrees → 18 percent
Blue slopes: 25 degrees → 47 percent
Black slopes: 40 degrees → 84 percent
Double-black slopes: 60 degrees → 173 percent

End-of-Unit Project

Teaching Insight

You may want to choose a student to read the poster instructions aloud and discuss questions students may have. As an early reminder, to prepare for the in-class work session, the teacher will need to gather poster paper, pens, and yard/meter sticks for student use in Lesson 9.

Additional Problems

6.4 More Real Slopes

a. 17 degrees
b. 5 degrees
c. 56 degrees

6.5 Ratios from Angles

a. 47 percent
b. 1143 percent

6.6 Handicapped Access Ramps

A slope of $\frac{1}{12}$ is 8.3 percent or 5 degrees to the nearest whole degree. Therefore, the only slope in the list that is less than $\frac{1}{12}$ is answer b, $\frac{4}{50}$.

6.7 Do Slopes Have Length?

A discussion about this problem may clear up some student misconceptions. When introduced to a new concept, novices sometimes focus on the wrong attribute, in this case, the length of the rays instead of the amount of turn. Students need to understand slope as being independent of line segment length.

6.8 Optional: Tangents

You may want to use this problem if you think your students would be curious about what the TAN button on the calculator is used for.

The idea is tangent (slope angle) = slope ratio; or put another way, inverse tangent (slope ratio) = slope angle. For example, in problem 6.3, Ski Slopes, a slope of 10 degrees is a slope ratio of tan(10°) = .176 . . . $\cong$ 18 percent and a 60-degree slope is a slope ratio of tan(60°) = 1.73 . . . = 173 percent grade.

Mental Math Start-up

Mental math answers are not included. Instead, teachers are encouraged to figure out these answers mentally for themselves. When we do mental math along with our students, we understand better what is going on in our students' brains, and our own mental math abilities improve, too.

When discussing the solutions, encourage students to share their own methods as well as listen to your methods. Be patient and don't force your students to use a particular method even though it may be more efficient. Students will remember methods they understand far better than methods that are mastered only by rote.

Teaching Insight

To introduce today's in-class tasks you could again add a mental math problem about slope: "Which is steeper, a line with slope two or a line with slope one-half?"

Teaching Insights

Core Problems are designed to be appropriate for student presentation. See Chapter 3, "Teaching Using Student Presentations," for steps to teaching these using a system of student presentations.

The problems in this lesson connect the idea of slope ratio and rate of change. For a line on a graph, slope and rate of change are the same only when the x- and y-axes are calibrated in the same-size units. For more insights, see Chapter 5, "Understanding Slope and Rate of Change."

7.1 Straights and Curves

Note: Example 2 is a magnification of what's in the circle in Example 1.

a. parabola
b. linear: $y = x + 3$
c. parabola
d. linear: $y = -.5x - 5$

7.2 One of These Things Is Not Like the Others

The "odd one out" for each row is as follows:

Row A: Intercepts. Intercepts should be $(-\frac{1}{2}, 0)$ and $(0, 1)$.
Row B: Rate of change. Rate of change should be $-\frac{2}{3}$.
Row C: Graph. The graph shows a slope of $\frac{1}{4}$. It needs to be redrawn to go through $(0, 0)$ and $(1, 4)$.

End-of-Unit Project

Teaching Insights

As the teacher you should circulate, recording partners' names and the situation each individual or team will use for their Linear Equation Poster. (See "From the Classroom: Choosing Partners" below for further insights.)

Again, remember to get ready for the in-class work session that happens in Lesson 9 by gathering poster paper, pens, and yard/meter sticks.

From the Classroom: Choosing Partners

In Lesson 7, students needed to choose their end-of-unit project partner and brainstorm a situation. I wanted to make sure students started thinking about their poster right away, so as groups worked on the lesson's core problems, I circulated with a sheet listing students' names, attached to a clipboard. I asked students whom they were partnering with and what the theme of their poster might be. I recorded their answers next to their names on the list.

When I got to Jackson, he casually listed his partners: "Mary and Ellie will be my partners. The three of us will work on the poster together."

I clarified the project's requirements. "This poster isn't a three-person project, Jackson. You can work with one other person, or alone."

Jackson whined, "But why not? We are all good friends and we don't want to work with anybody else. Mr. B., why can't the three of us work together, *please*?"

I reiterated the requirements. "No. This is a one- or two-person project. The amount of work to produce a good poster only requires one or two people. With three people working, someone would have to be sitting around doing nothing. Now you wouldn't want that, would you?"

Jackson was relentless. "But Mr. B., can't you make an exception? Aren't we your favorite students? We promise we will all work hard and make a really great poster together. And if you don't let the three of us work together, then we won't make a poster at all. Why are you so mean to us?"

I patiently listened, then decided to apply the project to the bigger picture. "Here's the deal, Jackson. When you graduate and get a job, you'll probably have a boss. He or she will assign you tasks and also tell you whom you are working with. Here in school, the poster is your work, and I'm the boss. Two of you can work together and the other person can either work alone or get someone else to partner with. If you want, I can find another person for you."

Jackson grumbled, then reluctantly agreed. "Well, okay. I'll work with Arnold."

I made note of this; in a later class, in which we did a similar end-of-unit project, I decided to avoid arguing. Rather than letting students choose partners, I randomly assigned each student a partner (just like the world of work outside the classroom). As a teacher, you'll need to make these types of decisions. In the classroom, you are the boss.

Additional Problems

Teaching Insight

Additional Problems are designed to be appropriate as homework or additional in-class work. Similar to the Core Problems, their answers can be presented through student presentations. See Chapter 3, "Teaching Using Student Presentations," for steps to teaching these using a system of student presentations.

7.3 Ordering Slopes

The only angle involved is 45 degrees, which corresponds to a slope of 100 percent, or 1. All the other slopes can be put into decimal form and then easily compared. From least steep to steepest:

| 45 percent | 0.5 | $\frac{7}{12}$ | 3 in 5 | 45 degrees | 120 percent |

7.4 Which One Doesn't Belong?

The odd one out for each row is as follows:

Row D: Slope. Slope should be –3.
Row E: Graph. The graph should go through (0, –3) and (2, 0).
Row F: x-intercept. The x-intercept should be at (6, 0).

Quiz B Answers

Assessing Lessons 4–7

Mental Math

Mental math answers are not included. Instead, teachers are encouraged to figure out these answers mentally for themselves. When we do mental math along with our students, we understand better what is going on in our students' brains, and our own mental math abilities improve, too.

Problems

5. Darling started at 2,000 pounds and is losing 18 pounds per week. The formula for her weight is $y = 2000 - 8x$. Sampson started at 800 pounds and is gaining 44 pounds a week. The formula for his weight is $y = 800 + 44x$. Their weights will be equal when $2000 - 8x = 800 + 44x$. Solving this equation gives $x = 19.35$. They will weigh the same sometime during week 19.

6. The horizontal line is $Y_1 = 3$. The other two lines are $Y_2 = (\frac{3}{5})x$ and $Y_3 = (-\frac{3}{4})x$.

7. The 20 percent grade can be sketched by first drawing a horizontal segment ten centimeters long. Then at one end of the segment, draw a vertical segment two centimeters long. Finally, draw the hypotenuse of this triangle to show a road with a grade of 20 percent. Measuring the slope angle from horizontal with a protractor should give about 11 degrees. But since this is a drawing, any value between 10 and 12 degrees could be counted as correct.

8 Answers and Teaching Insights

Mental Math Start-up

Mental math answers are not included. Instead, teachers are encouraged to figure out these answers mentally for themselves. When we do mental math along with our students, we understand better what is going on in our students' brains, and our own mental math abilities improve, too.

When discussing the solutions, encourage students to share their own methods as well as listen to your methods. Be patient and don't force your students to use a particular method even though it may be more efficient. Students will remember methods they understand far better than methods that are mastered only by rote.

Teaching Insight

When discussing answers to mental math problems 4 and 5, it should come out that zero must be substituted for y in order to get the x-intercept and zero substituted for x in order to get the y-intercept.

Core Problems

Teaching Insights

Core Problems are designed to be appropriate for student presentation. See Chapter 3, "Teaching Using Student Presentations," for steps to teaching these using a system of student presentations.

As groups work on Lesson 8's Core Problems, they should make especially sure that everyone in their group understands how to do each problem. These problems are similar to those that will be on the in-class assessment. In Lesson 9, have students present answers to these problems in addition to giving students time to work on their posters and unit summaries. You may want to devote more than one class period for Lesson 9. You could also develop your own review problem set for students to work on.

8.1 Baby Jakey's Weight

If the trend continues, Jakey will weigh 20 pounds after 20 weeks. Either write a table and extend it, or solve the formula y = $\frac{3}{4}$x + 5 *for* y = 20 *to get* x = 20.

8.2 Filling a Hot Tub

The water will reach a depth of 22 inches after 41 minutes. The equation is y = 0.5x + 1.5. **Note:** At the start there is already 1.5 inches of water in the tub!

8.3 Calculator Designs

Design 1. Four equations $y = mx + b$ all with the same negative value for m, and the values for b at equal intervals.

Design 2. Four equations $y = mx + b$ with two having positive values for m, two having negative values for m, and all having the same value for b: $b = 2$.

8.4 Solving Equations

    a. $x = 9$ **b.** $x = 2.3$ **c.** $x = 18$

End-of-Unit Project

Teaching Insights

In the process of getting organized, students should essentially be making a small-scale prototype poster. The prototype should include data, a completed graph, a table, and an equation for their chosen situation. For the in-class poster work in Lesson 9, don't give students poster paper until you've signed off on their prototype poster. This step saves students—and you—a lot of headaches and paper!

To get ready for the in-class work session that happens in Lesson 9, you will need to provide poster paper, pens, and yard/meter sticks.

From the Classroom: A Reminder About the Test

During Lesson 8, I reminded students that they would be working on posters in class during Lesson 9. In Lesson 10, they would be taking an in-class unit assessment.

Kalusha raised her hand. "Can we have a group test?"

"No. I want to give you the chance to show me what you have learned and can do all by yourself."

Jackson piped in. "But what's going to be on the test?"

"The problems will be just like the ones we've been doing in these lessons. If you can do the Lesson 8 problems yourself, you'll do fine. Also, in Lesson 9 you'll write a one-page unit summary. You can use this summary during the test and hand it in as part of your grade."

Imani, a cheerleader, realized there was a conflict: "Mr. B., didn't you hear that Principal Skinner scheduled a big pep rally for this period on Friday? We won't be here to take the test."

"No. I didn't hear that. Well, if we have to go to the pep rally, then we will take the test on Monday."

My other math class periods weren't having a pep rally on Friday. But to be fair, I decided to have all my classes take the test Monday. These things happen. Sometimes you have to make on-the-spot adjustments. Flexibility is key.

8.5 Jerico

There are several possibilities for rate of population change depending on which data is used. A good argument can be made for choices 1 or 2 below.

Option 1. **a.** From 1985 to 2005, the population increased by 3.95 thousands per year.
          b. The equation for population is $y = 3.95x + 239$, where x is the years past 1985.
          c. This equation predicts a population of 337.75 thousand.

Option 2. **a.** From 1995 to 2005, the rate was 3.7 thousands per year.
          b. The equation for population is $y = 3.7x + 281$ where x is the years past 1995.
          c. This equation predicts a population of 336.5 thousand in 2010.

8.6 Turtle Race

This classic problem can be done in many ways: graphically, algebraically, or using plain arithmetic. The key idea is that each turtle travels at a constant rate throughout the race. If no students solve this problem, encourage them to keep working. You might want to assign it as an extra-credit problem.

One solution: Turtle B was 3 meters ahead of turtle C when turtle A finished. Twelve meters later, when turtle B finished, he was 5 meters ahead of turtle C. Therefore turtle B gained 2 meters on turtle C during the last 12 meters. Since both turtles ran at a constant rate, this means that every 6 meters that turtle B ran, he gained 1 meter on turtle C. Since turtle B beat C by 5 meters, the race must have been $6 \times 5 = 30$ meters long.

8.7 Equation, Graph, Slope, Intercepts

Row G: Graph goes through (0, –2) and (1, 1). Slope is 3; x-intercept at $\frac{2}{3}$, y-intercept at –2.
Row H: Equation is $y = \frac{3}{2}x - 1$. Slope is 1.5; x-intercept at $\frac{2}{3}$, y-intercept at –1.
Row I: Equation is $y = -.5x$. Graph goes through (0, 0) and (2, –1).

9 Answers and Teaching Insights

Note: Lesson 9 may take more than one class period.

Mental Math Start-up

Mental math answers are not included. Instead, teachers are encouraged to figure out these answers mentally for themselves. When we do mental math along with our students, we understand better what is going on in our students' brains, and our own mental math abilities improve, too.

When discussing the solutions, encourage students to share their own methods as well as listen to your methods. Be patient and don't force your students to use a particular method even though it may be more efficient. Students will remember methods they understand far better than methods that are mastered only by rote.

Teaching Insight

Remind students that there will be five mental math problems on Lesson 10's end-of-unit assessment. The mental math problems will be similar to those in this lesson.

End-of-Unit Project

Teaching Insights

For the Linear Equation Poster, provide poster paper, marker pens, and yard/meter sticks. You may want to have students rearrange their desks or tables so they have plenty of space to work on their posters.

Give a piece of poster paper to each pair only after you've checked their prototype poster. Some students who have planned well may be done before the period ends. If possible, put their posters up on the walls or windows as they finish.

Before the end of class, you should decide what you want to do about students who aren't yet finished. Options include requesting that students come in at lunch or after school to finish; take their poster home and finish it (due at the beginning of Lesson 10); or hand it in and accept a grade "as is."

Ten minutes before the end of class, let students know what they should do if they haven't finished. Collect the markers and posters. If time allows, finish the lesson with mental math.

From the Classroom: The Linear Equation Poster

For the poster part of Lesson 9, Brent and Lisa immediately wanted pens and poster paper to start their poster. However, they hadn't yet shown me preliminary data.

"You still don't have your prototype poster checked off," I reminded them.

"But we don't want to do it twice. Just give us the poster paper now and we'll do a good job the first time," Brent and Lisa pleaded.

"No," I firmly stated. "No prototype. No poster paper. Finish your prototype."

About fifteen minutes later, Brent and Lisa called me over to show me their data. "OK, Mr. B., here is what our poster will have on it."

Their paper included some poster details but did not contain a graph.

"I don't see a graph here," I pointed out.

"Do we have to?" Brent and Lisa whined.

"Yes. Just make a sketch of the graph. Then you can adjust the calibration on the axes to show off the data well on the poster." I knew from experience that when teaching adolescents, I needed to be firm with them about planning before doing. I answered a few more questions from Brent and Lisa. After a bit they brought me a decent graph. Then I gave them their poster paper.

One-Page Unit Summary

Teaching Insights

The one-page unit summary can be a requirement, optional, or omitted completely. If you choose to have your students do a summary, you could count it as 5 points toward a student's exam score.

The goal of making the summary is to help each student individually review and summarize the unit. Students who simply make a copy of someone else's notes or print out a computer page will not accomplish this goal. For this reason, you may want to require the summary to be in each student's own handwriting. Remember to collect the summaries with the unit assessment so students in later classes don't just trade summaries.

End-of-Unit Project

Teaching Insights: Sharing Completed Posters

Before class you'll need to put the posters up around the room so that all of the students can see them (I had to tape posters on the chalkboards and over the windows to get them all up). Tell students that their presentations should be brief, no more than three minutes. Students should point out the features of their poster so everyone can understand what they did. Most students will be proud to show off their work and enjoy seeing the work of others.

Another purpose of sharing is for students to get a realistic perspective of the quality of their own work. During sharing time, I suggest that you make no comments about quality, errors, craftsmanship, or grades. The time for constructive criticism is later, when you can talk to students individually.

Remind students that after sharing, they will be completing a self-evaluation for their own poster.

Teaching Insights: Evaluating Posters

After the sharing is done, pass out copies of the Linear Equation Poster Evaluation. Give one form to partners and one to each individual who worked alone. Depending on the time left in the class period, you can either have the students complete the form right then, or start them on the in-class unit assessment and collect the form the next class period.

After the Linear Relationships unit is over, I take down all the posters except for the best two or three from each class. I leave these best posters up for the rest of the year so students are reminded about what they learned during the unit.

From the Classroom: Poster Presentations

Kayla and Jackson stood before their poster at the front of the classroom, obviously proud to show it off. The title of their poster was "Cats on Diets." It gave a first impression of being nicely laid out. Kayla was a talented artist and had drawn a fat cat and a skinny cat on each side.

As they pointed out the features of their poster, I noticed that the rate of change in the numbers on one of their tables didn't agree with the m in the equation. Even though their poster was aesthetically appealing, getting the math correct was essential. I made a mental note to discuss this with Kayla and Jackson at a later time, during the poster grading process.

Next up were Arnold and Casey. Their poster was about catching fish and throwing them back into the water. Although their situation wasn't realistic and didn't make a lot of sense, all the required poster features were there and all the math was correct. I appreciated the creativity.

Spud and Fin were next. Their theme addressed saving and spending money. Neither student's handwriting was great and their poster had a lot of white correction fluid spots where they "messed up." They didn't get all the craftsmanship points, but everything else was fine.

Steven stood by his poster. He had insisted on doing his poster by himself and told me several times that making the poster was a "stupid assignment." He'd decided to use a video game as his situation. It was difficult to make sense of the poster, and clear that he hadn't put much effort into his work. He would get a poor grade on his poster. I knew Steven preferred assessment by written exams, and usually did well on them. On the other hand, some of the students who made outstanding posters found written exams stressful and always did poorly on them. Having both a poster and a written exam as final assessments gave me a clearer picture as to what these adolescents learned and could do after finishing this unit.

For the One-Page Unit Summary, you have several options from which to choose depending on your students and your own personal preferences.

We continued sharing posters. After everyone had shared, I passed out the Linear Equation Poster Evaluations. I knew that students would have a much more realistic idea about the quality of their own work after seeing the work of others. Later, when I graded the posters, I was pleased to see that the points I gave agreed closely with the points the students gave themselves.

Unit Assessment

Allow a minimum of forty-five minutes in class for each student to complete the written end-of-unit assessment. This exam provides an opportunity for students to show what they have learned and can do. Each student should work alone to complete the exam, using only their calculator and their brain. A few more suggestions:

☐ Do not let students take the exam as a group or with a partner.

☐ During the exam, leave posters up on the walls for students to see and/or allow students to refer to their notes.

Mental Math

Mental math answers are not included. Instead, teachers are encouraged to figure out these answers mentally for themselves. When we do mental math along with our students, we understand better what is going on in our students' brains, and our own mental math abilities improve, too.

Problems

6. about 22 degrees

7. **a.** $\frac{1}{30}$ gallon per mile   **b.** $y = -\frac{1}{30}x + 12$

8.

   a. $y = 128x + 4350$
   b. $y = -205x + 9640$
   c. Solve $128x + 4350 = -205x + 9640$; get $x = 15.89$ years. Therefore, the populations will be the same sometime in 2015, both about 6,384.

9. Solutions (without steps shown) are:

   a. $x = 26$ **b.** $x = 4.5$ **c.** $x = 4$

10.

   ☐ One pair is $Y_1 = m_1 x$ and $Y_2 = m_1 x + 4$ with slope $m_1 > 0$.
   ☐ The other pair is $Y_3 = m_2 x$ and $Y_4 = m_2 x + 4$ with slope $m_2 < 0$.

11.

   a. First segment: $\frac{5}{6}$ feet/second; second segment $6\frac{1}{3}$ feet/second(EA)
   b. Arnold walked 50 feet in 18 seconds, so $2\frac{7}{9}$ feet/second.

12. **a.** 68 inches to start   **b.** 27.2 minutes

13. When $x = 30$, $y = 102$.

References

Black, Paul J., and Dylan Wiliam. 1998. "Assessment and Classroom Learning." *Assessment in Education* 5 (1): 7–74.

Boaler, Jo. 2008. *What's Math Got to Do with It?* New York: Viking Penguin Group.

Edelman, Gerald M. 1993. *Bright Air, Brilliant Fire: On the Matter of the Mind.* New York: Basic Books.

Lawrence, Ann, and Charlie Hennessy. 2002. *Lessons for Algebraic Thinking, Grades 6–8.* Sausalito, CA: Math Solutions.

National Council of Teachers of Mathematics. 2000. *Principles and Standards for School Mathematics.* Reston, VA: The National Council of Teachers of Mathematics.

Zull, James E. 2002. *The Art of Changing the Brain: Enriching the Practice of Teaching by Exploring the Biology of Learning.* Sterling, VA: Stylus Publishing.

Dan Brutlag has more than thirty years of experience in curriculum writing and teaching mathematics at the middle school, high school, and university levels. Contact Dan at dan@meaningfulmath.com.